Microcomputers in Education: A Handbook of Resources

Edited by Katherine Clay

Preface by LeRoy Finkel

ORYX PRESS
1982

The rare Arabian Oryx is believed to have inspired the myth of the unicorn. This desert antelope became virtually extinct in the early 1960s. At that time several groups of international conservationists arranged to have 9 animals sent to the Phoenix Zoo to be the nucleus of a captive breeding herd. Today the Oryx population is nearing 300 and herds have been returned to reserves in Israel, Jordan, and Oman.

Copyright © 1982 by
The Oryx Press
2214 North Central at Encanto
Phoenix, Arizona 85004

Published simultaneously in Canada

Printed and Bound in the United States of America

Library of Congress Cataloging in Publication Data

Clay, Katherine.
  Microcomputers in education.

  Includes index.
    1. Education—Data processing—Handbooks, manuals, etc. 2. Computer-assisted instruction—Handbooks, manuals, etc. 3. Computer managed instruction—Handbooks, manuals, etc. 4. Microcomputers—Handbooks, manuals, etc. I. Title.
  LB1028.43.C55   1982   370′.028′54   82-12596
  ISBN 0-89774-064-5

Table of Contents

Foreword

*"Prediction is very difficult,
especially about the future."*
Niels Bohr

Fact: Sales of microcomputers to schools in 1981 totaled approximately $35 million.
Prediction: By 1984, microcomputer sales to schools will be $145 million, an increase of 314 percent.

Fact: Computer literacy is a catch-all term that has come to mean anything from familiarity with computers and their social impact to the ability to program computers.
Prediction: There will continue to be clashes between advocates of computer literacy and advocates of the traditional basic skills.

Fact: Major popular, noneducation-oriented magazines, such as *Time* and *Newsweek,* have recently featured stories on the impact of computers on education.
Prediction: The chasm between the computer literate and the computer illiterate will become greater (information stamps for the information poor?).

Fact: By the summer of 1981, three million micros (over-all—not just to schools) had been sold. Computer sales (not just micros) totaled $2.6 billion.
Prediction: By 1985, the computer industry will have sales totaling $62 billion.

Fact: In 1980, 50 percent of U.S. workers were employed in some aspect of the information industry.
Prediction: Kindergarten children today may have a potential life expectancy of 100–125 years; by the year 2000, 80 percent of the working population of the U.S. may be employed in the information industry; roughly half of today's jobs will change drastically or disappear altogether.

Fact: The documents cited in this resource guide probably contain more than anyone wants to know about micro-computers.
Prediction: By reading the citations in this resource guide, you can become familiar with the impact of microcomputers on education; by reading the documents themselves, you can advance one step further toward becoming computer literate.

Preface

The field of computer education is growing and changing so rapidly that interested beginners are hard pressed to know where to look to learn about the topic. Conversely, those of us who have been "at it" for some time are inundated daily with a plethora of materials that include new product news, software information and reviews, "how to" books and articles, resource lists, lists of new organizations, curriculum guides, and a wealth of other information. To catch up now and learn what you need to know so that you can use computers successfully in your schools is only part of the task that confronts you. To keep abreast of the field so that you, your staff, and your instructional program can continue to grow as new developments appear is the true challenge.

This resource guide will help you in your effort to bring yourself "up-to-speed" in the field of computer education. It will put you in touch with the literature, the organizations, the people, and the resources that will keep you abreast of the current state of the art in computer education as that state changes, and it does change with alarming regularity.

Here, between two covers, you have past, present, and future commentary on the state of the art. You have references to past articles and past research from which you can gain valuable insight, ideas, and knowledge that, hopefully, will inhibit your need to reinvent the wheel. Included are current articles, current organizations, and current resources that can give you insight into the growth that has taken place over the years. And, within these pages, is reference to the future, the controversies, and the perceived problems that may befall the field, included so that you can be aware and be wary.

It's all here . . . between these covers.

LeRoy Finkel
Instructional Computing Coordinator
San Mateo County Office of Education
Redwood City, CA

How to Use this Guide

The best advice I can give the user of this guide is to read this section because it will aid in understanding the layout of the book and in getting the most out of it. The section organization looks straightforward—and it is—but understanding the philosophy *behind* the organization might be of help.

Because the literature on microcomputers is multi-faceted, there are many overlapping areas. For example, a description of a teacher education class which is designed to teach teachers to evaluate microcomputer hardware and software could logically fall into the "Teacher Education" or "Selection/Evaluation Criteria" sections of this guide. In such a case, a somewhat subjective decision was made, based on the content of the document at hand, as to whether the entry focused more on "how to conduct a teacher education course" (in which case it was placed in the "Teacher/Administrator Education" section), or on "how to evaluate" (in which case it was placed in the "Selection/Evaluation Criteria" section). Actually, it may take as much daring and creative thinking to use this resource guide as it does to become computer literate. Browse. You might be pleasantly surprised.

Grade level was another problem area in organizing this book. Many times, a document would discuss a computer literacy unit in a high school where the grade level seemed almost immaterial to the unit. In this case, the citation was placed in the "Computer Literacy" section but was not listed in the index under "High School Students." In another instance, a document describing a unit for teaching computer literacy to kindergarten children was placed in the "Computer Literacy" section because it's unusual to teach computer literacy to kindergarten children. However, it was *also* listed in the index under "Kindergarten Children."

The index term "fund raising" did not fit into any of the sections exclusively, so projects which describe how parents raised funds for buying computers for their child's school or how someone collected spare parts to build a microcomputer for his/her child's school, were placed in the "References/Resources" section—a resource for figuring out how to do it. Stretching a point a bit, but where else should these citations go? There are many additional sources of information in the "References/Resources" section . . . "pointers to pointers" they're sometimes called. There are guides to additional resources, bibliographies which will provide more reading material for the serious student of microcomputers, and lists of lists—films, journals, texts, children's books about computers. All in all, probably more than any rational person wants or needs to know about microcomputers. The index has been provided for the reader's convenience in locating citations on specific issues or topics or questions.

Other overlapping areas are "Research Studies," "Management Applications," and "Libraries." This last title is not a section in itself but heavily represented in the index. What is the rationale behind the placement of a document on the cost effectiveness (Research Studies) of using a microcomputer to keep track of overdue library books (Management Applications) in an elementary school library? The rationale used in organizing this guide was mostly subjective. If a researcher might be interested in replicating the study, and enough detail was present to allow him/her to do so, the citation went into the "Research Studies" section. If an elementary school librarian might be interested in trying out such a program, and the document contained enough information to allow him/her to do so, the citation went into the "Management Applications" section.

With all this in mind, please use the section headings as general guides and the index as a more specific reference.

To round out this resource guide, an appendix, "Additional Sources of Information," is included and presents some additional sources of information: (1) computer journals; (2) catalogs and directories; (3) user groups; (4) associations; (5) computer science degrees; (6) microcomputer centers to visit; and (7) software sources.

The citations in this guide were compiled from computer searches of Educational Resources Information Center (ERIC); *Magazine Index* (in an attempt to ascertain what the general, noneducational literature was saying about microcomputers); *Newspaper Index* (for the same reason as *Magazine Index*); and from manual searches of *Education Index, Microcomputer Index,* and the extensive library and information files of the San Mateo Educational Resources Center (SMERC). At the time of compilation, DIALOG Information Services (a subsidiary of Lockheed) had announced the impending appearance of *Microcomputer Index* online, but the file was not yet available for computer searching in mid-May of 1982. Consequently, the corresponding hand catalog, rather than the computer file, was used in compiling this guide.

Because microcomputer literature seems to be growing in the same geometric proportion as microcomputers themselves, an arbitrary stopping point had to be set. For this guide, March 1982 was selected as the stopping point. There are no citations older than 1976 and none more current than March 1982.

Each section of this guide begins with a brief introduction. Within each section, citations are arranged by document format: journal and newspaper articles, microfiche documents, and books and reports. An order number prefaced by ''EJ'' plus the notation ''Reprint: UMI'' is present on certain entries. This indicates that a photocopy of the article may be purchased from:

> Article Copy Service—CIJE
> University Microfilms International
> 300 N. Zeeb Road
> Ann Arbor, MI 48106
> (800) 521-3042

All documents carrying an order number prefaced by ''ED'' plus the notation ''Reprint: EDRS'' are available from:

> ERIC Document Reproduction Service
> P.O. Box 190
> Arlington, VA 22210
> (703) 841-1212

A ''List of Acronyms'' is also included within this guide. Because so many acronyms are used within the field, computer terminology is becoming increasingly complex, often resembling alphabet soup. And while most initials within acronyms actually stand for words, others, such as LOGO and BASIC, are simply names of computer languages. Likewise, acronyms, such as TERAK, mean nothing, except that they serve as brand names for specific computer systems. In addition, some acronyms may have more than one representation or have been used for so long that many within the industry itself no longer know what such acronyms stand for. The glossary is an attempt to clarify certain standard acronyms that are used within the computer industry and throughout this book.

List of Acronyms

ACCOLADE: Alternative Curriculum for Computer Literacy Development

ACM: Association for Computing Machinery

AIDS: Assisted Instructional Development System

AIS: Advanced Instructional System

CAD: Computer Aided Design. Also Computer Assisted Dialog

CAI: Computer Assisted Instruction

CALE: Computer Augmented Learning Environment

CAUSE: Comprehensive Assistance to Undergraduate Science Education

CBE: Computer Based Education

CBT: Computer Based Training

CISS: Computerized Instructional Support System

CMI: Computer Managed Instruction

ECMI: Educational Computing in Minority Institutions

EDUNET: Educational Network

IEP: Individual Education Programs. Also Individualized Education Plan

JEM: Joint Educational Management

MECC: Minnesota Educational Computing Consortium

MICA: Management of Instruction with Computer Assistance

MICRO-CMI: Microcomputer Based System of Computer Managed Instruction

NAEP: National Assessment of Educational Progress

PLAN: Program for Learning in Accordance with Needs

PLATO: Programmed Learning for Automated Teaching Operations. Also Programmed Logic for Automatic Teaching Operations

TICCIT: Time-shared Interactive Computer Controlled Television

TIPS: Teaching Information Processing System

VDT: Video Display Terminal

Futures/Trends

This section runs the gamut from philosophical looks at what the future holds to very concrete analyses of the capabilities of the present-day computer, along with speculations about future trends and developments in computer technology. The section also includes overviews of the role and impact of computers and ideas on how to plan for the future.

Literature which addresses the future of education is almost as plentiful as literature which discusses microcomputers specifically. Obviously, the two are often intertwined. Futurist Ralph Taylor (*Compact,* Summer 1980, page 45) believes that, when schools and populations are expanding, emphasis is on building curriculum and finding new teachers; when times are austere, emphasis shifts to improving the curriculum and teachers already present in the educational system. Few would argue that times are austere for education today. Few would argue that schools need improvement. Many believe that using the technology made possible by the computer is one way of making this improvement. Others, like Arthur Shostak (*Phi Delta Kappan,* January 1981, page 356), believe that creating computer literates could be dangerous if the result is an even more divided society, with the elite at an advantage over those who lack the skill to use computers or the knowledge that computers can impart.

Whichever view is held by the reader—negative or positive—it would be difficult to deny that microcomputers are making a solid impact on the schools, as well as on society as a whole.

JOURNAL ARTICLES

1. **Classroom of the Future.** Nilson, Jeff. *Kilobaud: Microcomputing.* v5, n9, p36–40, Sep 1981.

   Presents the scenario of a classroom of the future, where one teacher, aided by computer technology, successfully teaches 55–60 students. The author feels, however, that certain conditions must change before this type of class organization can occur. He believes that software must be improved; a teacher shortage must develop, since teachers will not be fired to be replaced by computers; and the efficiency of computer assisted instruction in reading and language must be more widely accepted.

2. **The Coming Systems Break: Technology and Schools of the Future.** Shostak, Arthur B. *Phi Delta Kappan.* v62, n5, p356–59, Jan 1981.

   The terms "compunications" and "telematique" have been coined to cover the recent rapid advances in the integration of computers and information-handling technologies such as TV, radio, and electronic communications. Asserting that the "telematique" revolution brings as radical a change to education as did the first grammar book in 1492, the author considers possibilities for future educational delivery systems and for reforms which will bring the benefits to the masses, as well as to the elite.

3. **Computer Assisted Instruction in Agricultural Education.** Hudson, C. Jordan. *Agricultural Education Magazine.* v53, n2, p19–20, Aug 1980 (EJ 231 592; Reprint: UMI).

   The author discusses the impact of the computer on education and describes specific applications of automation for agricultural education, including drill and practice, testing, simulation, and student records maintenance.

4. **Computer-Assisted Instruction in Today's Reading Classroom.** Blanchard, Jay S. *Journal of Reading.* v23, n5, p430–34, Feb 1980 (EJ 225 383; Reprint: UMI).

   Reviews the development of computer assisted reading programs and predicts that, as costs decline and the quality of the educational program improves, more computers will be found in the classroom. Includes a discussion of bilingual CAI programs in Dallas and Los Angeles and the proposed satellite CAI delivery system in Alaska.

5. **Computer Makers Try to Lure Consumers by Touting Value of Educational Programs.** Herron, Vanessa. *Wall Street Journal,* Jul 16 1981.

   Discusses the poor software programs on the market and current attempts to improve them.

6. **Computers in Education: Future Projections.** Mogus, Mary Ann. *Interface Age.* v6, n12, p84–85, Dec 1981.

   Looks at the possibility of providing a microcomputer as an interactive, individualized instructional tool for every student.

7. **Computer Technology and Instruction: Implications for Instructional Designers.** Kurshan, Barbara. *Educational Technology*. v21, n8, p28–30, Aug 1981.

Presents some issues that instructional designers must be prepared to face in order to expect some degree of control over microcomputer usage for instructional purposes.

8. **Educational Computing—The Giant Awakes.** Prentice, Lloyd R. *Kilobaud: Microcomputing*. v5, n9, p86–88, 90–91, Sep 1981.

Using statistical surveys and interviews with educators and computer marketing personnel, the author presents data on the growth rate of computers in education, outlines ways they are being used, and considers two major problems which may slow this phenomenal growth rate. They are: budget cuts which could prevent hardware purchase and difficulties involved in supplying quality marketable software.

9. **Educational Technology—Fad or Educational Renaissance?** Benedict, Gary M. *NJEA Review*. v54, n9, p36–37, May 1981 (EJ 243 444; Reprint: UMI).

Looks at some of the learning benefits of having a computer at school and at home. Predicts expansion in all types of electronic technology.

10. **Educational Technology: The Next Ten Years.** Dede, Christopher J. *Instructional Innovator*. v25, n3, p17–23, Mar 1980.

The author predicts a severe economic crunch for education in the 1980s and suggests how five existing educational technologies (TV, instructional calculators, home computer terminals, videodiscs interfaced to personal computers, and electronic communications/information services) can be used to save money and to increase efficiency.

11. **Educators and the Knowledge Revolution.** Heise, David. *Educational Computer Magazine*. v1, n3, p30–31, Sep–Oct 1981.

The author challenges today's educator to play a crucial role in the new technology of knowledge administration by defining standards that any knowledge device should meet.

12. **FAR Futures of Computers in Education.** Garson, James W. *The Computing Teacher*. v7, n5, p36–40, Apr–May 1981.

Using a Stanford Research Institute scenario writing technique called FAR, the author generates five scenarios on the future uses of computers in education. From various ideas about our social, political, and economic future, he infers the types of computer programs that will be used in schools and the curricular areas they will cover. Some of the scenarios suggest a shift in education from the schools to the home.

13. **Hardware Considerations for Computer Based Education in the 1980's.** Hirschbuhl, John J. *Journal of Research and Development in Education*. v14, n1, p41–56, Fall 1980.

In the future, computers will be needed to sift through the vast proliferation of available information. Among new developments in computer technology are the videodisc microcomputers and holography. Predictions for future developments include laser libraries for the visually handicapped and CAD.

14. **How Manufacturers Are Selling Micros to Schools.** Wise, Deborah. *InfoWorld*. v3, n27, p18–19, Nov 23 1981.

Discusses the marketing approach to computers taken by Apple, Commodore, and Radio Shack.

15. **Into the 80's with Microcomputer-Based Learning.** Aiken, Robert M.; Braun, Ludwig. *Computer*. v13, n7, p11–16, Jul 1980.

Briefly reviews the development of microcomputers and their impact on education. Future applications in the classroom are discussed, as well as techniques to evaluate the effect of using microcomputer systems.

16. **Microcomputers: Tools of the Present and Future.** Lopez, Antonio M., Jr. *School Media Quarterly*. v9, n3, p164–67, Spr 1981 (EJ 247 480; Reprint: UMI).

Identifies commercially available microcomputer systems, briefly reviews the use of microcomputers in education, describes uses of computers in the home, and sketches the role of computers in libraries. Seven references are cited.

17. **Personal Computers: Putting a Finger on the Future.** Pepper, Gary. *Town and Country*. v136, n5021, p98–99, 151–52, 154, Jan 1982.

Presents, in easy-to-understand terms, an overview of the potential importance of the small computer in daily living. The author concludes that, although people may be able to get along without computers, they won't want to.

18. **Rushing toward Courseware.** Petrakos, Pamela. *80 Microcomputing*. n16, p74, 79–81, Apr 1981.

Looks at current efforts by several major textbook publishers to produce microcomputer based computer assisted instructional materials and discusses attitudes some of these publishing houses are taking toward the growing educational software market.

19. **School Computers Score at Last.** *Business Week*. v2, p66, 68, Jul 27 1981.

This article describes how microcomputers are being increasingly used in education. Includes numbers of units sold and gives projections to 1984 of the number of units that will be sold and their costs.

20. **Shift to Microcomputers.** *School Administrator*. v38, n6, p26–27, Jun 1981.

Presents a brief resume of a report detailing trends in microcomputer use in the schools. For the full report "Student Use of Computers in Schools," contact Jeanette Goor, National Center for Educational Statistics, Room 620, Presidential Building, 6525 Belcrest Road, Hyattsville, MD 20782.

21. **Society Will Balk, but the Future May Demand a Computer for Each Child.** Papert, Seymour. *Electronic Education*. v1, n1, p5–6, 31, Sep 1981.

In this essay, the author discusses his work with LOGO and argues that computers are tools which should be as commonplace as pencils and that very young children are both capable of and motivated by working with computers.

22. **Speech Peripherals Make Computers More Human.** *Personal Computing*. v5, n6, p19–20, 35–36, 38, 86, Jun 1981.

Several "talking" microcomputers are analyzed and their potential impact is evaluated. A vendor guide is included.

23. **State of Future Microcomputing.** Hogan, Thom. *InfoWorld*. v3, n20, p60–61, Oct 5 1981.

Predicts trends in growth in the microcomputer industry and suggests which companies might be entering the computer making industry in the near future.

24. **Tomorrow Has Arrived.** Wiegner, Kathleen K. *Forbes*. v129, n4, p111–15, 119, Feb 15 1982.

Presents, in layperson's terms, a look at the proliferation, costs, capabilities, and competition in the microcomputer industry.

25. **Two Views of Educational Technology in the Future.** Dede, Christopher J.; Bowman, Jim R. *Journal of Thought*. v16, n3, p111–18, Fall 1981 (EJ 251 863; Reprint: UMI).

Given all the possible participants (parents, governments, schools, the media, business) in implementing new information technologies in education, the authors present two extreme scenarios: (1) all participate to develop instructional technology, and (2) no one cooperates. Part of a theme issue on educational futures.

26. **Xerox's 820: No Surprises Here.** Lobello, Tony. *Electronic Education*. v1, n1, p18–20, Sep 1981.

The features and capabilities of the Xerox 820 microcomputer are described.

MICROFICHE

27. **Future Applications of Electronic Technology to Education.** Lewis, Arthur J., et al., Florida University, Gainesville, FL, Nov 1978, 36p. Sponsoring Agency: Florida State Department of Education, Tallahassee, FL (ED 206 260; Reprint: EDRS).

Developments in electronic technology that have improved and linked together telecommunication and computers are discussed, as well as their use in instruction, implications of this use, and associated issues. The first section briefly describes the following developments: microcomputers and microprocessors, bubble memory, lasers, holography, optic fibers, satellite-to-rooftop communications, videodiscs, charge-coupled devices, and the application of electronic technology to communication. The potential of these developments for education is then explored by showing how telecommunications and computers can be used in instructional programs as a source of information, a source of dynamic interaction, or resources for managing instruction. The possible impact of electronic technology on educational aims and content is also discussed, as well as the question of when and where electronic technology will be used in education. A bibliography of 29 items is included.

28. **Long-Term Electronic Technology Trends: Forecasted Impacts on Education.** Paper presented to Congress of the United States, House of Representatives, Committee on Education and Labor, Subcommittee on Elementary, Secondary, and Vocational Education (April 25, 1979). Joseph, Earl C. Apr 1979, 18 p (ED 179 878; Reprint: EDRS).

The evolving "silicon revolution" is producing a seemingly endless list of new electronic technology poised at the threshold for massive application throughout society. Such an evolution includes the expectation for transforming elementary, secondary, and vocational education for both the short-term and long-term futures. The major new thrust is the emergence and growth of "smart machines." Technology for education includes embedding increasingly capable, but physically small, microprocessor logic; digital storage/memory; sensors; communications circuits and links; and eventually voice-actuated and reply mechanisms for creating convivially smart machines which are more humanistic for students. As modern technology advances, the synergistic relationship between humans and machines allows us to do more with less. This new human-machine symbiosis will change most institutions in society, including education.

29. **Microcomputers in Education. Report No. 4798.** Feurzeig, W., et al., Bolt, Beranak and Newman, Inc., Cambridge, MA, Oct 1981, 115p. Sponsoring Agency: Ministerio para Desarollo de la Inteligencia Humana, Caracas, Venezuela; National Institute of Education (DHEW), Washington, DC (ED 208 901; Reprint: EDRS).

A brief summary of the history of computer assisted instruction and discussion of the current and potential roles of microcomputers in education introduce this review of the capabilities of state-of-the-art microcomputers. Discusses currently available software for them and speculates about future trends and developments. A survey of current applications of microcomputers is followed by descriptions of hardware capabilities, including input and output devices and displays, as well as memory. Reviews some representative software for teaching mathematics, language skills, social sciences, natural sciences, and educational games. The status of research on the instructional effectiveness of CAI is briefly discussed, and five prominent studies which show consistent results are cited. Descriptions of near-future technological capabilities include hardware trends, software developments (high-level languages, operating systems, and user interface), artificial intelligence, and programing languages. Changing expectations, potential problems, and educational promise are addressed in a concluding discussion of prospects and pitfalls. A 43-item bibliography is provided.

30. **Microcomputers in the Schools: New Directions for British Columbia. Discussion Paper Number 05/80.** Wright, Annette, British Columbia Department of Education, Victoria, BC, Canada. Information Service, JEM Research, Victoria, BC, May 1980, 42p (ED 208 846; Reprint: EDRS).

This summary of the Instructional Use of Microcomputers Scope Document, dated February 22, 1980, outlines short-term plans for the educational use of microcomputers in British Columbia, indicates long-term possibilities, and describes current project activities. The project comprises two major phases: (1) continued field liaison and research and (2) curriculum integration and development. Hardware is discussed in terms of educational uses, the context of application, urban or rural location, and educational level. The fourfold approach to software involves the development of a standards manual for evaluation of courseware; modification of courseware by JEM Research; development of new programs; and development of teacher programs by teachers themselves. Inservice training for teachers will be provided, and the exchange of information concerning project efforts will take place through a newsletter and discussion papers. The integration and implementation of microcomputers into the provincial curriculum is described through a series of diagrams, including a curriculum development model, an advisory structure, schedules for K-12 curriculum development and implementation, long-range development and assessment, implementation plans and sequence of development tasks, a production model of microcomputer based courses, and the overall plan. The appendices include requirements analysis of available microcomputers and descriptions of authoring languages.

31. Microelectronics at Work: Productivity and Jobs in the World Economy. Worldwatch Paper 39. Colin, Norman, Worldwatch Institute, Washington, DC, Oct 1980, 64p (ED 192 144; Reprint: EDRS).

A combination of revitalized employment policies, greater industrial democracy, and new ways of distributing both the hours of work and the fruits of technological change are essential if the benefits of the microelectronic revolution are to be equitably shared. Microelectronic technology promises an array of benefits, and the electronic age is already well under way. As it progresses during the last two decades of the twentieth century, it will lead to improvements in productivity in factories and offices; changes in the way information is processed, stored, and communicated; and alterations in the content of many jobs.

Differing rates of development of the electronics industry may lead to shifting advantages of competition in the international marketplace. Like all major technological changes, the transition to microelectronics will raise difficult political issues, among which the impact on jobs and employment is most prominent.

32. More Hands for Teachers. Report of the Commissioner's Advisory Committee on Instructional Computing. Florida State Department of Education, Tallahassee, FL, Feb 1980, 39p (ED 191 120; Reprint: EDRS; also available from Educational Computing Pro-

ject, Department of Education, Knott Building, Tallahassee, FL 32301. Copies of the complete 226-page report may be obtained from the Educational Products Distribution Center, Department of Education, Room B-10-A Collins Building, Tallahassee, FL 32301).

This overview of the role and impact of computers on education and instruction examines: (1) computing applications for instruction, types of computer systems for instructional computing, and current instructional computing uses; (2) planning for future implementation of instructional computing, management concerns, and implementation issues; and (3) instructional computing costs, cost effectiveness analysis, and comparative costs of computer systems for computer assisted instruction. The conclusions and recommendations of the report concern the assumptions on which Florida public policy should be based, policy formulation, priorities for the implementation of policies, and support of the policy implementation. References are listed.

BOOKS

33. The Micro Millennium. Evans, Christopher. New York: The Viking Press, 1979, 225p.

Although this book is about computers, no technological knowledge or insight is necessary to follow the arguments presented. The author predicts that society will undergo traumatic changes in the course of reaping the benefits of the microprocessor. His vision includes the collapse of the work ethic, the erosion of the power of the professions, and the coming of the cashless society. Also predicted are sweeping social and psychological changes. The author divides the future into short-term (1980-82), middle-term (1983-90), and long-term (1991-2000) as he analyzes the impact of the computer.

34. Running Wild, the Next Industrial Revolution. Osborne, Adam. Berkeley, CA: Osborne/McGraw-Hill, 1979, 18p.

The author suggests that understanding the facts behind the advancement of microelectronics could make the difference between the future becoming a dream or a nightmare. Presented is a prediction of events of the next decade: roughly half of today's jobs will change drastically or disappear altogether; robots will take over assembly line jobs from blue-collar workers; microelectronics devices will peform many white-color duties; new technology will usher in the miracles of bionics, increase communications and make real every person's dream of more leisure than labor; and new horizons for computer crime will be opened.

Computer Literacy

In one respect, this entire resource guide deals with the topic of computer literacy, and so there is a good deal of overlap between this section and other sections, such as "Philosophy" which philosophically looks at the need or rationale for computer literacy, and "Classroom Applications" which deals with implementing computer literacy programs in the schools.

In this section, an attempt is made to focus on what computer literacy is, how a school, district, or state becomes computer literate, various definitions of computer literacy, and on when or how to go about making a population computer literate. If the document at hand seemed to contain enough information on goals or objectives or scope and sequence to implement the program, it was placed in the "Classroom Applications" section. Many brief program and project descriptions are found in this computer literacy section; more substantive descriptions will be found in the "Classroom Applications" section.

JOURNAL ARTICLES

35. **An Alternative Curriculum for Computer Literacy Development.** Denenberg, Stewart A. *AEDS Journal.* v13, n2, p156–73, Win 1980 (EJ 223 597; Reprint: UMI).

    This paper describes the ACCOLADE system in terms of its design goals, its components, an illustrative session with a learner, the computer managed instruction subsystem, and a brief evaluation of a model pilot study.

36. **Are You a Computer 'Illiterate'?** Jay, Timothy B. *The Computing Teacher.* v8, n4, p58–60, 1980–81.

    The author presents a definition of computer literacy and suggests ways of becoming computer literate.

37. **Back to Basics, Forward to Computing?** Birmingham, Jason. *Personal Computing.* v6, n3, p23–24, Mar 1982.

    The author suggests that, if computer literacy is to take place with the three R's, it must be introduced to children early in their grammar school years.

38. **A Case for Universal Computer Literacy.** Eisele, James E. *Journal of Research and Development in Education.* v14, n1, p84–89, Fall 1980 (EJ 237 813; Reprint: UMI).

    Presents a rationale for and definition of computer literacy. Lists goals and program objectives in the areas of understanding and operating computers, systematic problem solving, and computers in society. Briefly discusses program implementation.

39. **Classrooms Make Friends with Computers.** Ankers, Joan, et al. *Instructor.* v89, n7, p52–56, 58, Feb 1980 (EJ 219 066; Reprint: UMI).

    Part one of a two-part feature on computers includes explanations of: what a computer is, how a computer works, a miniunit to introduce computers into the curriculum, a kooky computer quiz, computer applications, computer use in several schools, and computer careers.

40. **Computer Literacy—1985.** Brumbaugh, Kenneth E. *The Computing Teacher.* v8, n4, p49–50, 1980–81.

    Looks at current curriculum development projects in computer literacy and argues for an individualized, learner-based approach.

41. **Computer Literacy—What Is It?** Johnson, David C. *Mathematics Teacher.* v73, n2, p91–96, Feb 1980 (EJ 218 393; Reprint: UMI).

    Computer Literacy Objectives developed by the MECC computer literacy study are given. They are grouped under six headings: "Hardware"; "Programing and Algorithms"; "Software and Data Processing"; "Applications"; "Impact"; and "Attitudes, Values, and Motivation."

42. **Computer Literacy: What Is It?** Johnson, Mildred Fitzgerald. *Business Education Forum.* v35, n3, p18–22, Dec 1980 (EJ 235 922; Reprint UMI).

    Discusses philosophy, facts, and opinions regarding the definition of computer literacy. Presents suggested computer literacy course content and recommends delivery systems or methodologies that can be used for instructional purposes.

43. **Computerphobia: What to Do About It.** Jay, Timothy B. *Educational Technology.* v21, n1, p47–48, Jan 1981.

    Considers the symptoms, causes, and remedies of computer phobia among educators. Outlines an introductory seminar on computing.

44. Computers Blossom at a Small School in Iowa.
Lockard, James. *Instructional Innovator.* v25, n6, p25, 48, Sep 1980.

Discusses how a small private college integrated computer literacy into its curriculum.

45. Computers May Help Basic Skill Students Improve Their Status. Wild, Jane H. *Electronic Education.* v1, n1, p27–28, Sep 1981.

Evidence suggests that the use of computers with college-level students who have poor basic skills can be successful. The need for computer literacy for both students and teachers is stressed.

46. Computer Training for the Real World. *American School and University.* v53, n8, p60–61, Apr 1981 (EJ 247 054; Reprint: UMI).

Hull High School in suburban Boston, Massachusetts is rated as one of the top 10 secondary schools in the country offering a computer education program. The same computers used by the students are shared by school officials for administrative tasks.

47. Computer Tutors: An Innovative Approach to Computer Literacy. Part I: The Early Stages. Targ, Joan. *Educational Computer Magazine.* v1, n1, p8–10, May–Jun 1981 (Available from P.O. Box 535, Cupertino, CA 95015).

In part one of this two-part article, the author describes the evolution of the ''Computer Tutor'' project in Palo Alto, California and the strategies she incorporated into a successful student-taught computer literacy program.

48. Compu-Tots and Other Joys of Museum Life.
Hirshberg, Peter. *Instructional Innovator.* v26, n6, p28–30, Sep 1981.

Capitol Children's Museum in Washington, DC has created a Future Center classroom stocked with 20 Atari 800 microcomputers. It offers free public access and nine courses, ranging from ''Compu-Tots'' (for preschoolers and their parents) to ''An Introduction to Programming'' (for adults). The program's operation, educational orientation, and software approach are discussed.

49. A Conceptual Framework for Developing Computer Literacy Instruction. Anderson, Ronald E.; Klassen, Daniel L. *AEDS Journal.* v14, n3, p128–50, Spr 1981.

Ten years ago, ''computer literacy'' was an unknown phrase; now it is widely discussed and many companies are developing related instructional materials. A conceptual framework is offered for the delineation of computer literacy, with a list of eight topics: applications, hardware, impact, limitations, programing, software and information processing, usage, and values.

50. Educational Pilot Program: Every Child with a PET. Holman, Elli. *Personal Computing.* v6, n2, p76–77, Feb 1982.

Reports on the two-year-old experiment at Lawton Elementary in Ann Arbor, Michigan to integrate personal computers into all disciplines and at all grade levels.

51. Elevated Education Made Easy: Computers in Schools. Esbensen, Thorwald. *Personal Computing.* v5, n8, p93, 95–97, Oct 1981.

Provides advice to concerned citizens and educators on getting personal computers into the schools.

52. From Classroom to Commerce: How Computer-Literate Teachers are Making Their Skills Pay Off. Calkins, Andrew. *Electronic Learning.* v1, n1, p42–45, Sep–Oct 1981.

Four routes for computer literate teachers to take—from teaching business and industry—are presented.

53. The Future of Computer Education: Invincible Innovation or Transitory Transformation? Gress, Eileen K. *The Computing Teacher.* v9, n1, p39–42, Sep 1981.

Presents a strong case for the need for computer literacy and a description of some problems which will be encountered in developing curriculum.

54. Instructional Use of Microcomputers. Daneliuk, Carl; Wright, Annette E. *Education Canada.* v21, n3, p4–11, Fall 1981.

The centralized, provincewide approach used to introduce microcomputers into the public school system of British Columbia is described. The rationale of the project; inservice, coordination, and information efforts; hardware and courseware acquisition; and field testing are discussed.

55. In This System, the Computer Future Is Now. Levin, Dan. *American School Board Journal.* v169, n3, p27–28, Mar 1982.

Describes two high school campuses where virtually all 3,800 students and 275 teachers are computer literate.

56. The Lawrence Hall of Science: Teaching Personal Computing in the Hills of Berkeley. Morgan, Chris. *onComputing.* v2, n2, p13–19, Fall 1980 (EJ 229 349; Reprint: UMI).

The Lawrence Hall, a science museum and teaching center in Berkeley, California, is providing thousands of students and teachers with hands-on experience with personal computers. This article describes how Lawrence Hall promotes computer awareness and provides science instruction through microcomputer controlled interactive museum exhibits.

57. Linking Computer to Curriculum Starts with the Teacher. Roberts, Harold Pepper. *Educational Computer Magazine.* v1, n1, p27–28, May-Jun 1981 (Available from P.O. Box 535, Cupertino, CA 95015).

Clover Park School District has planned a two-year phased-in implementation of microcomputers. This article describes the successes and problems encountered in the first year of the program, which focused on teacher training.

58. Microcomputers in the Elementary School. Smith, Lucia Walker. *CMLEA Journal.* v3, n2, p7–8, Spr 1980.

Describes the Computer Corner in the library of Stonegate Elementary School and the six-week computer course developed for fourth- and fifth-grade gifted students.

59. One State's Approach to Computer Literacy.
Kirchner, Alice M. *Technological Horizons in Education.* v8, n4, p43–44, May 1981 (EJ 252 831; Reprint: UMI).

Reports on a pilot project to present an introductory course in computer literacy for elementary through postsecondary students in Pennsylvania. Includes descriptions of course rationale and teacher training.

60. Planning for Computer Education—Problems and Opportunities for Administrators. Luehrmann, Arthur. *NASSP Bulletin.* v65, n444, p62–69, Apr 1981.

The author discusses the myriad problems created by the need for computers in today's education but concludes it can be a satisfying experience for a school principal to oversee the birth and growth of new courses in computing.

61. Sesame Place: Learning, Playing, and Using Computers. Bove, Tony; Rhodes, Cheryl. *Recreational Computing.* v9, n6, p8–14, May–Jun 1981.

Sesame Place is a unique family theme park in Bucks County, Pennsylvania which combines a physical playground with a conceptual playground where children can learn on their own by interacting with computers and science experiments. This article describes the park's approach to computer literacy and education through play for children of all ages.

62. Space Age Multi-CPU Computer Network Is Just for Fun and Education, Too. *Technological Horizons in Education.* v7, n6, p43, Nov 1980.

Describes the Sesame Place's Computer Gallery. With 56 Apple II computers linked by three Nestar Cluster/One Model A hard disc systems, it is the first commercial permanent education play park. Programs for this hands-on, indoor/outdoor park, as well as a description of the facility, are given.

63. Star Your Microcomputer in a Classroom Drama.
Ehrenborg, John D. *Educational Computer Magazine.* v1, n3, p45–47, Sep–Oct 1981.

Drama is used as an effective tool for teaching computer literacy in an elementary school. Pictures accompany the article.

64. There's a Microcomputer in Your Future. Souviney, Randall. *Teacher.* v97, n5, p53–58, Feb 1980 (EJ 226 889; Reprint: UMI).

The author provides an introduction to microcomputers in the schools by answering the type of questions a teacher without computer background might ask, such as "What is a computer?"; "What is a microcomputer?"; and "How can I teach children to program?"

65. Through a New Looking Glass. Olds, Henry F., Jr. *Kilobaud: Microcomputing.* v5, n9, p62–64, 67–74, Sep 1981.

The author discusses the fears teachers develop when faced with the need to become computer literate and to integrate computers into the classroom. He suggests some ways of making the computer seem less threatening.

66. A Visit to a School at which Every Student Learns to Compute. Mace, Scott. *InfoWorld.* v3, n27, p14, 28, Nov 23 1981.

A report on the schoolwide computer program for grades five through eight offered at Crittenden Middle School in Mountain View, California. With 15 PET/CBM microcomputers, every student receives a two-week programing course, and software packages are being used in many school subjects.

67. Why Be a Computer Literate? Jay, Timothy B. *Thrust.* v10, n3, p25–27, Jan–Feb 1981.

The author defines some of the basic components, objectives, and benefits of computer literacy instruction.

MICROFICHE

68. Computer Literacy. Hunter, Beverly. Apr 27, 1981, 13p. Paper presented at the Patterns Conference on Computer Literacy (Rochester, NY, Apr 27–28, 1981) (ED 207 617; Reprint: EDRS).

The concept of computer literacy is examined as it applies to two-year colleges. The paper begins with definitions of the term, emphasizing the skills, knowledge, and attitudes toward computers that are considered criteria for computer literacy. The paper continues by describing a conference at which educators attempted to visualize the technology of the future and its implications and lists areas in which these educators were successful (e.g., predicting the intelligent videodisc) and unsuccessful. Next, six reasons why a broad base of computer literacy is needed are examined, including reasons related to the changing economy; the changing nature of jobs; promotion of equity in access to computers; world competition; the need to encourage student skills; and the need to understand issues of public policy for technology. The paper then suggests priorities for planning computer literacy programs. Suggestions, in order of importance, include: enhancing the computer literacy of educational administrators; planning curricula for the use of the computer; purchasing hardware and software to support the curricula; supporting faculty members who encourage computer literacy; supporting academic computing facilities; gaining assistance from industry; and fostering computer literacy at precollege levels. The paper concludes with a projected profile of the computer literacy level of the entering college class of 1985, which foresees a wide variation in student experience with computers.

69. Computer Literacy in Higher Education. AAHE—ERIC/Higher Education Research Report No. 6, 1981. Masat, Francis E., American Association for Higher Education, Washington, DC; ERIC Clearinghouse on Higher Education, Washington, DC, 1981, 63p. Sponsoring Agency: National Institute of Education (ED), Washington, DC (ED 214 446; Reprint: EDRS).

Computer literacy in higher education and its relationship to computer science and other areas of the institution, such as general and continuing education, are considered, along with issues related to academic and administrative aspects of computer literacy. The impact of microcomputers is assessed, as is the extent to which computer science and literacy are increasing in other countries. It is suggested that given the continuing success of computer literacy at the elementary and secondary levels, computer literacy in higher education could, in time, acquire the status of a basic skill. Curricular concerns include the advantages and disadvantages of computer assisted instruction (CAI), the relationship of microcomputers to CAI, and who should be computer literate. According to the literature, computer literacy is intended for everyone, and the literacy level that is effective at the institution may be inappropriate at another, although common characteristics are indicated. Important administrative considerations are the issues of facilities planning, the acquisition of computer literate faculty and staff, and the cost of providing literacy to students, faculty, and administrators.

In brief, the relationships among goals of students, faculty, and staff members and the relationship of these goals and resource support are determining factors in the planning, development, and implementation of computer literacy programs. Issues and problems of national scope that require national strategies for their resolution include: networks, national databases, federal support of computer education, national cooperation and coordination, and international competition. The state of the art in computer literacy practices and research is renewed, and the bibliography is appended.

70. **Computer Literacy Program Brief.** Human Resources Research Organization, Alexandria, VA, 1978, 20p. Sponsoring Agency: National Science Foundation, Washington, DC (ED 193 022; Reprint: EDRS).

Computer Literacy Program Briefs for seven schools and/or school districts are presented. Topics covered in each brief include: the institution or institutions covered; the educational program strategies; the target student audience; major components of the instructional program; illustrative examples of specific objectives; organization of the instructional package; facilities and equipment used; the nature and extent of teacher training; classroom activities and resource materials; and the impact and effect of the computer literacy program.

71. **Course Goals in Computer Education, K-12.** Allenbrand, Bob, ed., et al., Tri-County Goal Development Project, Portland, OR, 1979, 217p. Sponsoring Agency: Oregon State Department of Education, Salem, OR; Washington Office of the State Superintendent of Public Instruction, Olympia, WA; (ED 194 074; Reprint: EDRS; also available from Commercial-Educational Distributing Services, P.O. Box 8723, Portland, OR 97208).

Designed to be used in conjunction with a school district's educational goals and focusing on what is to be learned, rather than the methodology to be used, the program and course goals presented here are intended as guidelines for planning and evaluating elementary and secondary school curricula in computer education. Of four possible goal levels, only program (general outcomes) and course (specific outcomes) goals are included, leaving the use of behavioral and/or planning objectives optional at the classroom teacher level. Two taxonomies are provided: (1) description of the three types of goals in this collection—knowledge (information), process (skills and abilities), and values (attitudes and opinions); and (2) classification of a specific subject (computer education) into components (e.g, computer systems, hardware, software, applications). Program goals are listed for both career and computer education, and course goals are given for values and computer education,

processes of inquiry and problem solving, basic education and computer education, computer systems, calculators, computer hardware, computer software, computer applications, computer uses in business and industry, history of computer development, computer science, and computer education and careers. A concept list, an index to computer related issues, and a subject index are attached.

72. **Desk Top Computers.** Merchant, Ronald. Jan 1981, 7p. Paper presented at the National Conference on Educational Alternatives for a Changing Society (Miami, FL, Jan 28–30, 1981) (ED 200 275; Reprint: EDRS).

Investigations conducted by Spokane Falls Community College (SFCC) indicate that introductory computer courses for business students should emphasize the elimination of "computer phobia" through the provision of hands-on experience. In a survey of over 160 area businesses, SFCC found that 53 percent of the respondents ranked hands-on experience as the most desirable form of instruction: 37 percent indicated that a combination of theory and experience was the most desirable form. In response to this employer need and in an effort to increase efficiency in terms of costs and student time, SFCC initiated a competency-based, one-credit "Introduction to Microcomputers" course. In this course, students utilize the TRS-80 Radio Shack computer in the college's Business/ Math Machines Center and complete exercises in flow charting, simple programing, data entry, data correction, and data retrieval. The course is offered on a continuous enrollment basis, and students complete assignments at their own pace, usually within 15 hours. After one year of implementation, the course has proven to be both an effective hands-on complement to computer theory courses and a useful core class for business students who do not need substantial theoretical instruction to effectively use the computer as a tool. This descriptive report concludes with short answers to seven questions about course management and equipment.

73. **Developing a Computer Literate Faculty at College of DuPage.** Carlson, Bart, Interuniversity Communications Council (EDUCOM), Princeton, NJ, 1980, 10p. Paper presented at the Annual Meeting of EDUCOM (1980) (ED 203 835; Reprint: EDRS).

Until 1978, academic and administrative departments at College of DuPage, an Illinois community college, bought computer related equipment and software without an overall plan or coordination. The development of a coordination plan focused on finding an internal mechanism to solve the problems of individual departments buying computer related products, and the inability to forecast accurately over an eight-year period how much computer time would be needed by each department. A formal long-range plan was developed that described the mission, philosophy, goals, and history of the college and the computer services section and discussed computing industry trends. It concluded that the college's best course of action was to invest in commercially developed and maintained software, rather than in a larger staff. Both maxicomputer and minicomputer systems of varied types and brands comprise the current college system. Other features of the plan include computer awareness training for staff, a monthly newsletter, and a microcomputer laboratory to allow faculty to experiment with hardware and software. Areas of benefit to the college found in the planning process included: awareness throughout the institution of the need for planning; campuswide compatibility for interconnection to maxicomputers and microcomputers on campus and within the national educational computer network (EDUNET); ease in problem determination; ease in coordinating maintenance; and institutional awareness of what is happening at the department levels.

74. Developing Standards and Norms for Computer Literacy. Discussion Paper 06/80. Wright, Annette, British Columbia Department of Education, Victoria, BC, Canada. Information Service, JEM Research, Victoria, BC, Canada, Jul 1980, 75p (ED 208 847; Reprint: EDRS).

This paper provides educators with a general perspective on computer literacy and an in-depth examination of the Computer Literacy Awareness Assessment, conducted by MECC. Addressing computer literacy as part of the ongoing use of computers in a classroom setting is identified as the most reasonable approach for introducing computer literacy to British Columbia. Computer literacy is then defined and discussed in terms of specific experiences or desired outcomes of literacy. The remainder of the paper discusses the development of the assessment, including purposes of the test and its structure. The test consists of three parts: (1) affective assessment with six scales of five items each; (2) cognitive test of 53 true/false or multiple choice items; and (3) survey of background variables with 37 items. The appendices include: validation of the test; administration and scoring norms; a prior cognitive subtest; revised cognitive subtests; reliabilities, means, and standard deviations for cognitive subtests; intercorrelations and percentile norms of cognitive subtest and revised subtest; affective scales; and Computer Literacy Questionnaire.

75. Microcomputers in Education: Getting Started. Conference Proceedings (Tempe, Arizona, January 16–17, 1981). Watson, Nancy A., ed., Arizona State University, Tempe, AZ. College of Education, Jan 1981, 349p. Legibility varies (ED 205 216; Reprint: EDRS; also available from Gary Bitter, Arizona State University, Payne 203, Tempe, AZ 85281).

Included in these proceedings are brief write-ups of many of the 55 presentations given at a conference for elementary and secondary teachers and administrators. The conference emphasized using microcomputer technology in elementary education, secondary education, special education, and administration. General interest sessions were also held. The keynote addresses, entitled ''The Challenge of the 80's: Computer Literacy,'' was given by Dr. Andrew Molnar of the National Science Foundation. Sessions focused on: computer literacy: computer assisted instruction in the basic skill areas at elementary and secondary levels: applications for microcomputers in special education and gifted education; methods of evaluating microcomputer systems; hardware and software comparisons; career education and guidance information systems; instructional techniques for teaching BASIC programing language to elementary and secondary students; ways of designing computer proposals for federal funding; and microcomputers in the Fine Arts areas. Appended is a bibliography of BASIC computer books and lists of computer journals, film companies producing films about computers, microcomputer manufacturers, and software vendors.

76. A Teacher's Introduction to Educational Computing. The Illinois Series on Educational Application of Computers, No. 2e. Dennis, J. Richard, Illinois University, Urbana, IL. Department of Secondary Education, 1979, 18p. Sponsoring Agency: EXXON Education Foundation, New York, NY (ED 183 182; Reprint: EDRS).

This paper is designed to provide the educator with an overview of instructional applications of the computer, along with important issues related to each application. Applications discussed include: computer managed instruction, drill and practice, simulation, computer assisted testing, instructional games, tutorials, problems solving and classroom management. Some ways that teachers have started bringing computers into their schools are listed, as well as two references. This is one of a series of monographs prepared as resources for the preservice and inservice training of teachers.

BOOKS

77. Are You Computer Literate? Billings, Karen; Moursund, David. Salem, OR: Math Learning Center, 1979, 148p.

This book does not assume that the reader has had any previous experience with computers nor does it require that any particular computer equipment be available. It covers the following topics: ''What Is a Computer?''; ''Why Do Computers Exist?''; ''Data Entry and Computer Programming''; ''Smart Machines''; ''How Computers Are Being Used''; ''How Computers Affect People''; ''What Else Is There to Know''; and ''Additional Resources.'' A computer literacy exam is appended. Illustrated.

78. Be a Computer Literate. Ball, Marion; Charp, Sylvia. Morristown, NJ: Creative Computing Press, 1977, 61p.

Presents, in very simple language, a discussion of what computers are, what kinds of computers exist, and what goes on inside a computer. Includes instructions for writing a simple program and a brief glossary.

79. Computer Awareness Book. Spencer, Donald D.; Beatty, John H. Ormond Beach, FL: Camelot Publishing Company, 1978, 32p.

This coloring book is designed to help primary children learn basic concepts about computer applications, flow charting, and programing.

80. An Introduction to Computers and Computing. Rogers, Jean B. Eugene, OR: University of Oregon (International Council for Computers in Education, Department of Computer and Information Science), 1981, 48p.

This booklet provides a general outline for the topics which might be covered in a computers and computing course at the secondary school level. It delineates the topics to be presented, provides a timeline, and includes a resource list for teachers.

Philosophy

Philosophy is a difficult topic to deal with in a resource guide such as this. A philosophical treatise (Philosophy) on why teachers need educating (Teacher Education) about the power, capabilities, and time-saving nature (Management Applications) of microcomputers would be placed in the "Philosophy," "Teacher Education," or "Management Applications" sections, depending on the document's emphasis. Many subjective judgments were made.

"Philosophy," in this section, is defined rather loosely. Opinion papers will be found here, as well as learning theories and philosophical looks at the impact of computers. There is a good deal of overlap between this section and the "Futures/Trends" section. There are also a number of documents dealing with the issues of overcoming resistance to the micro; of using micros with special populations, such as handicapped or gifted students; and the motivational value of simulating games for both special populations and the nonexceptional student. Entries concerning problems with software and other obstacles faced by the micro industry are found in this section, as are entries dealing with the difficulties in providing enough hardware for hands-on experience with microcomputers.

There is even some overlap between this section and the "Research" section when a review and synthesis of the literature, for example, is made and presented along with the author's views on the topic. Again, an attempt was made to analyze the focus, depth, intent, or emphasis of the document at hand.

JOURNAL ARTICLES

81. **The Authoring System: Interface Between Author and Computer.** Pogue, Richard E. *Journal of Research and Development in Education.* v14, n1, p57–68, Fall 1980.

    The purpose of this paper is to present a philosophy of approach for guiding the design and implementation of computer based systems for the authoring of CAI lessons.

82. **The Brain and the Machine.** Matheson, Willard E. *Personal Computing.* v2, n4, p37–45, Apr 1978.

    The human brain and a computer are compared. The author concludes that there will be a hand-in-hand relationship between humans and machine in the future, with the computer extending humans' mental capabilities.

83. **The Classroom Computer Is Naked.** Lambert, Frank L. *Interface Age.* v6, n3, p84–89, Mar 1982.

    The author warns against jumping onto the microcomputer bandwagon without first thoroughly investigating hardware and software.

84. **The Coming of Computer Literacy: Are We Prepared for It?** Molnar, Andrew R. *Educational Technology.* v21, n1, p26–28, Jan 1981 (EJ 240 913; Reprint: UMI).

    Offers an overview of issues pertaining to societal readiness to cope with the information explosion. The need for computer literacy, an examination of computers in education, and the role of the National Science Foundation in computer literacy programs are discussed.

85. **The Computer and Basic Math Instructor: The Promise and the Problem.** Wagner, William J. *Classroom Computer News.* v1, n5, p18–19, May 1981.

    Argues that, while many programs are available in the area of K-8 mathematics, what is needed is a set of coherent, sequenced packages and more systematic planning for instructional computing.

86. **Computer-Based Exploratory Learning Systems for Communication-Handicapped Children.** Geoffrion, Leo D.; Goldenberg, E. Paul. *Journal of Special Education.* v15, n3, p325–32, Fall 1981.

    A rationale for exploratory learning via computers is presented, emphasizing the need for modeling normal communication development in children with communication handicaps, including deafness, cerebral palsy, and autism.

87. **Computer Illiteracy—A National Crisis and a Solution for It.** Luehrmann, Arthur. *Byte.* v5, n7, p98, 101–02, Jul 1980.

    Citing the critical need for computer literacy instruction, the author looks at the obstacles to developing computer education and the necessary steps for accomplishing it.

88. **The Computer in Education: Myth and Reality.** Grinstein, Louise S.; Yarmish, Rina J. *Educational Horizons.* v59, n4, p158–64, Sum 1981 (EJ 250 731; Reprint: UMI).

    To explode seven common myths about computers in the classroom, the authors explore some of the limitations and strengths of computers in education. They conclude that the computer should not be shunned as a "bogeyman" but should be used as an aid in achieving the overall goals of education.

89. Computer Literacy in Grades K-8. Hunter, Beverly. *Journal of Educational Technology Systems.* v10, n1, p59–66, 1981-82.

A rationale is presented for an approach to computer literacy in which computer related objectives are integrated into language arts, math, science, and social studies curricula. A set of objectives for developing instructional sequences using computers is given. Four references are listed.

90. Computer Literacy: The Fourth Basic Skill? Kitch, Dale. *Business Education Forum.* v35, n2, p22–23, Nov 1980 (EJ 235 818; Reprint UMI).

Stresses the need to improve the design of data processing curricula and to help students understand how technology affects human development and career choice.

91. Computer Literacy—What Should it Be? Luehrmann, Arthur. *Mathematics Teacher.* v74, n9, p682–86, Dec 1981.

Responding to MECC objectives found in the article "Computer Literacy—What is It?," the author argues that these objectives only indicate an "awareness" level of learning about computers, while computer literacy should mean "the ability to do computing." He discusses the problem of providing adequate hardware so that all students can have hands-on experience.

92. Computer Literacy—Who Needs It? Frenzel, Louis E. *Interface Age.* v6, n3, p38, 40, Mar 1981.

Defining computer literacy as the ability to program and apply computers to specific applications, the author questions whether public schools have the time and the money to teach it and whether technological advances won't soon make programming obsolete anyway!

93. Computers and Computer Cultures. Papert, Seymour. *Creative Computing.* v7, n3, p82–92, Mar 1982 (EJ 244 587; Reprint: UMI).

Instruction using computers is viewed as different from most approaches to education, by allowing more than right or wrong answers; providing models for systematic procedures; shifting the boundary between formal and concrete processes; and influencing the development of thinking in many new ways.

94. Computers and Education: The Genie Is Out of the Bottle. Lautsch, John C. *Technological Horizons in Education.* v8, n2, p34–35, 39, Feb 1982 (EJ 252 817; Reprint: UMI).

Presents an overview of computer use in education and other realms. Concludes that the true computer revolution in education may not be the use of computer assisted instruction but, rather, the combining of computers with other electronic devices for widespread decentralized education.

95. Computers Are Objects to Think With. Hereford, Nancy-Jo. *Instructor.* v91, n7, p86–87, 89, Mar 1982.

In this interview with Seymour Papert, Papert tells teachers why they shouldn't wait to become acquainted with computers.

96. Computers Can Teach Where Others Fail. Howe, J.A. *Technological Horizons in Education.* v8, n1, p44–45, Jan 1981 (EJ 252 811; Reprint: UMI).

Describes the use of computers in special education to provide new learning opportunities and better teaching strategies for handicapped students. Indicates that computers can teach cursive writing, test the effectiveness of a teaching method, and simulate systems such as tune composition and sentence generation.

97. Computer Simulation Games. Ahl, David H. *Teacher.* v97, n5, p60–61, Feb 1980.

Several simulation games are described, and a case is made for the motivational value of using microcomputers for game playing.

98. Computer Simulations in the Classroom. Noonan, Larry. *Creative Computing.* v7, n10, p132, 134, 136, 138, Oct 1981.

A middle-grades educator discusses the educational value of computer simulations and explains how to introduce them into the classroom. The example he uses is a TRS-80 Level II social studies simulation "Santa Paravia and Fiumaccio," which is about two fictional countries.

99. Coping Strategies for Resistance to Microcomputers. Townsend, Barbara; Hale, Deborah. *T.H.E. Journal.* v8, n6, p49–50, 52, Nov 1981.

Presents a number of strategies for overcoming resistance to the introduction of microcomputers into the classroom.

100. Developing Computer Literacy in Children: Some Observations and Suggestions. Holzman, Thomas G.; Glaser, Robert. *Educational Technology.* v17, n8, p5–11, Aug 1977 (EJ 166 381; Reprint: UMI).

Presents a study of the kinds of computer programs children write and the types of programing concepts with which they have difficulty.

101. Education and Technology: The Changing Basics. Allen, Dwight W.; McCullough, Lawrence N. *Educational Technology.* v20, n1, p47–53, Jan 1980 (EJ 216 491; Reprint: UMI).

Notes the changing role of technology in education and society. Explores the increased use of educational technology brought about by its sophisticated simplicity; the need for new skills in society that technology can supply; and the humanizing, freeing effect of technology mastery for the user.

102. Education, Computers and Micro-Electronics. Lewis, R. *Technological Horizons in Education.* v8, n1, p47–49, Jan 1981 (EJ 252 813; Reprint: UMI).

Traces general educational changes over the last 20 years, summarizes past and present uses of computers in education, and identifies the impact microelectronics will have on present and future education. Discusses vocational training, availability of inexpensive educational resources, teaching methods, and teacher education.

103. Guidelines for Developing Basic Skills Instructional Materials for Use with Microcomputer Technology. Caldwell, Robert M. *Educational Technology*. v20, n10, p7–12, Oct 1980.

The purpose of this article is to present specific guidelines for designing instructional programs that will be delivered on microcomputers, so that these programs will tap the capacity of a microcomputer system in such a way that users will develop a range of cognitive skills and evolve useful learning strategies.

104. Here's What Classroom Computers Can Do. Stewart, L. R. *American School Board Journal*. v169, n3, p32, Mar 1982.

Presents ideas for using microcomputers in both academic and management areas.

105. How Can Microcomputers Help? Hope, Mary. *Special Education: Forward Trends*. v7, n4, p14–16, Dec 1980 (EJ 240 541; Reprint: UMI).

The author asks 16 questions regarding the use of microelectronics in special education. Areas addressed are: overall contribution of microelectronic aids; a framework for thinking about microelectronics in special education; teacher training, information, and equipment; communication aids; and priorities.

106. How Should Schools Use Computers? Stewart, George. *Popular Computing*. v1, n2, p104, 106, 108, Dec 1981.

Looks at four current issues in the computers-in-education debate: (1) Is the computer a tool or a new subject? (2) Is computer assisted instruction an appropriate use of computers? (3) Should computer literacy be taught and, if so, what should be taught and by whom? and (4) What equipment should be purchased?

107. How to Set Up a Computer Environment. Coburn, Peter, et al. *Classroom Computer News*. v2, n3, p29–31, 48, Jan–Feb 1982.

This article, excerpted from *Practical Guide to Computers in Education*, states that the most important consideration in creating a computer environment in a school is winning over reluctant teachers, followed closely by placing computers in the best location for use in that school.

108. Impact of Personal Computing on Education. McIsaac, Donald N. *AEDS Journal*. v13, n1, p7–15, Fall 1979 (EJ 223 568; Reprint: UMI).

Describes microcomputers, outlines lessons learned from the evolution of other technologies as they apply to the development of the microcomputer, discusses computer literacy as a problem-solving tool, and speculates about microcomputer use in instruction and administration.

109. Information Technology for Education: An Agenda for the 80's. Melmed, Arthur S. *Technological Horizons in Education*. v7, n6, p46–47, 62, Nov 1980.

Describes technologies applicable for educational use, including computers, calculators, video storage, and word processing devices. Applications of the new technologies to basic skills in reading and comprehension are given. Three goals for the 1980s, resulting from new information technologies, are suggested.

110. Introducing Instructional Computing into the Educational Environment. Pritchard, William H., Jr. *Electronic Education*. v1, n1, p15, 21–24, 30, Sep 1981.

Presents a 10-step model for successfully reaching the goal of full implementation of computerized instruction.

111. Issues in the Evaluation of Instructional Computing Programs. Wagner, Walter. *Educational Computer Magazine*. v1, n3, p20–22, Sep–Oct 1981.

The purpose of this article is to review some of the assumptions underlying software authoring guides and evaluation instruments and to discuss some of their strengths and weaknesses.

112. The Microcomputer as a Participant in Educational Simulations. Brownlee, Elliott. *The Computing Teacher*. v9, n1, p11–12, Sep 1981.

Discusses a computer simulation game which deals with the problem of recidivism or ex-convicts returning to a life of crime. In this game, the microcomputer acts as a participant or tutor—roles which the author believes are best for microcomputers in education.

113. Microcomputers: Impact on Society and Education. Alexander, Wilma Jean. *Business Education Forum*. v35, n8, p19–21, May 1981 (EJ 245 276; Reprint: UMI).

Discusses the role and importance of computers in today's society. Business teachers must prepare their students to function in an environment which includes all kinds of computers.

114. Microcomputers in Education: A Concept-Oriented Approach. Wolfe, George. *Byte*. v6, n6, p146, 150, 152, 154, 158, 160, Jun 1981.

It is suggested that the technology that possesses the greatest potential to transform society and human life is the microcomputer.

115. Microcomputers in Education: The State of the Art. Gleason, Gerald T. *Educational Technology*. v21, n3, p7–18, Mar 1981 (EJ 244 284; Reprint: UMI).

This overview of instructional applications of computer assisted instruction and microcomputer applications discusses current developments in hardware and software; the need for independent review and evaluation of CAI programs; then growing importance of computer literacy, especially for teachers; and projections for the future. Eleven references are listed.

116. Microcomputers in Social Studies: An Innovative Technology for Instruction. Saltinski, Ronald. *Educational Technology*. v21, n1, p29–32, Jan 1981 (EJ 240 914; Reprint: UMI).

Examines the application of microcomputer statistics in social studies and computer access and simulations in middle school environments. An interdisciplinary framework of curricula among social studies, science, and mathematics teachers with equal access to microcomputers and software programs is encouraged.

117. Microcomputers in the Classroom. Price, Camille C. *Mathematics Teacher.* v71, n5, 425–72, May 1978 (EJ 182 213; Reprint: UMI).

The definition of a microcomputer, along with examples and resource information for such systems, the advantages of microcomputer kits, and the value of the microcomputers to the student, are discussed.

118. Microcomputers: Out of the Toy Chest and into the Classroom. Levin, Dan. *Executive Educator.* v2, n3, p19–21, Mar 1980.

Briefly outlines the positions some schools have taken on the use of microcomputers as teaching devices.

119. Microcomputers Will Not Solve the Computers-in-Education Problem. Moursund, David. *AEDS Journal.* v13, n1, p31–39, Fall 1979 (EJ 223 570; Reprint: UMI).

Discusses barriers to computer use in instruction and outlines the program of the Elementary and Secondary School Subcommittee of the Association for Computing Machinery to identify and lay a foundation for the solution of problem areas.

120. Microcomputer Systems for Authoring, Diagnosis, and Instruction in Rule-Based Subject Matter. Scandura, Joseph M. *Educational Technology.* v21, n1, p13–19, Jan 1981 (EJ 240 912; Reprint: UMI).

Argues that microcomputers are inexpensive, reliable, and sufficiently powerful to meet important educational demands and that with authoring/driver systems, educators could make far greater use of what is known about cognitive processes, especially structural learning.

121. The Micro in the Media Center. Konopatzke, Pat. *Educational Computer Magazine.* v1, n2, p8–9, Jul–Aug 1981.

The reasons behind the decision to put microcomputers into the media center are presented.

122. Microliteracy, School Administrators and Survival. Mathews, Walter M.; Winkle, Linda Wyrick. *Compact.* v15, n3, p22–23, 37, Fall 1981.

Presents a strong case for the need for computer literacy for administrators first—then teachers and students.

123. The Micros Are Coming. Miller, Inabeth. *Media and Methods.* v16, n7, p32–35, 72, 74, Apr 1980.

The author suggests that some sobering questions be contemplated: "What are microcomputers?"; What can they do?"; What are the problems involved?"; and "How can educators maintain control over their introduction and use in the schools?"

124. The Next Great Crisis in American Education: Computer Literacy. Molnar, Andrew R. *Journal of Technological Horizons in Education.* v5, n4, p35–38, 1978.

Discusses the importance of the computer in today's complex society. Argues strongly in favor of integrating the computer into education by introducing computer related curricula at all levels of education and thus developing a computer literate society.

125. Once More—A Computer Revolution. Weizenbaum, Joseph. *Bulletin of the Atomic Scientists.* v34, n7, p12–19, Sep 1978 (EJ 187 639; Reprint: UMI).

Discusses what limits should be placed on the application of computers to human affairs and the importance of knowing the impact of computers on human dignity.

126. On Effective Documentation. Robinson, Michael. *Creative Computing.* v6, n11, p30–32, Nov 1980 (EJ 239 245; Reprint: UMI).

Discusses the nature and importance of effective documentation in computer programing.

127. Personal Computers: The Golden Mean in Education. Esbensen, Thorwald. *Personal Computing.* v5, n11, p115–16, 120, Nov 1981.

Discusses three microcomputer applications being used in Minnesota elementary schools: (1) drill and practice; (2) computer literacy; and (3) educational games. The author addresses common criticisms of each application.

128. Profile of Change in Education: A High School Uses Microcomputers. Grossnickle, Donald R.; Laird, Bruce A. *Educational Technology,* v21, n12, p7–11, Dec 1981.

This article is intended to report the paths and pitfalls associated with introducing microcomputers into a secondary school.

129. Programs for Preschoolers: Starting Out Young. Kimmel, Stephen. *Creative Computing.* v7, n10, p44, 46, 50, 53, Oct 1981.

From his experiences with his small son, the author gives advice on the types of computer games most suitable for very young children.

130. The Role of Personal Computer Systems in Education. Bork, Alfred; Franklin, Stephen D. *AEDS Journal.* v13, n1, p17–30, Fall 1979 (EJ 223 569; Reprint: UMI).

Reviews the role of computers, particularly the personal computer, in the learning process; discusses the many ways of using the computer to assist learners; and considers the advantages of personal computers over time-sharing computers.

131. Seymour Papert: Spearheading the Computer Revolution. Nelson, Harold; Friedman, Rich. *onComputing.* v3, n1, p10–12, Sum 1981 (EJ 245 097; Reprint: UMI).

Discusses Seymour Papert's ideas about computers and their role in the educational process. Papert believes that present-day computers program, rather than teach, the child. He has developed a simple and fun computer language called LOGO, which lures children into learning by exploration and discovery.

132. Understanding How to Use Machines to Work Smarter in an Information Society. Molnar, Andrew R. *Technological Horizons in Education.* v7, n1, p42–46, Jan 1980.

Discusses the need, primarily by the education community, to improve computer literacy throughout every segment of the population in order to take advantage of the technological advancements. The ultimate goal is to increase worker productivity.

133. Who Are the Computer Kids? Grossman, Florence. *onComputing.* v3, n2, p24–25, Fall 1981.

The author looks at what self-taught computer whiz kids, primarily middle-class boys, find so fascinating about their hobby and what they accomplish with computers. She draws implications for schools about the motivational effects of computers and the need for teaching computer literacy.

MICROFICHE

134. Analysis of a Simple Computer Programming Language: Transactions, Prestatements, and Chunks. Report No. 79-2. Series in Learning and Cognition. Mayer, Richard E., California University, Santa Barbara, CA. Department of Psychology, 1979, 34p. Sponsoring Agency: National Science Foundation, Washington, DC (ED 207 549; Reprint: EDRS).

This discussion of the kind of knowledge acquired by a novice learning BASIC programing and how this knowledge may be most efficiently acquired suggests that people who do programing acquire three basic skills that are not obvious either in instruction or in traditional peformance: (1) the ability to analyze each statement into a type of prestatement, (2) the ability to enumerate the transactions involved for each prestatement, and (3) the ability to chunk prestatements into general clusters or configurations. The instructional implications of a psychological analysis of the basic concepts underlying performance in BASIC programing are considered, and an alternative instructional approach—the ''transactional approach''—is recommended for teaching programing. This approach involves teaching the underlying concepts of transactions, prestatements, and chunks, using a concrete model of the computer, before emphasizing hands-on learning. It is argued that, once the student has acquired the relevant subsuming concepts, the relationship between program and output will be more meaningful. Nine references are listed, and appendices include the eight levels of knowledge for BASIC and examples of transactions, prestatements, and chunks and diagrams of the traditional and transactional approaches. Other publications in this report series are listed.

135. An Approach to Integrating Computer Literacy into the K-8 Curriculum. Hunter, Beverly, Human Resources Research Organization, Alexandria, VA, Oct 1980, 12p. Based on a presentation for the National Educational Computer Conference (Norfolk; VA, Jun 24, 1980). Sponsoring Agency: National Sci-

ence Foundation, Washington, DC (ED 195 247; Reprint: EDRS).

The goal of the research and development project described is to make it possible for students in grades K-8 to acquire at least minimal computer related skills. The report gives the long-range goals of the project, perceptions on the need for a computer literacy program, recommendations of approaches for satisfying that need, and the pros and cons of a K-8 infusion approach to computer literacy. A series of curriculum guides for the K-8 computer literacy program, for use by school administrators, media center people, teachers for grades K-8, and subject coordinators, will be produced before the termination of the project, scheduled for September 1983.

136. Calculators and Microcomputers for Exceptional Children. Etlinger, Leonard E.; Ogletree, Earl J., 1981, 9p (ED 202 707; Reprint: EDRS).

The potential of using calculators and microcomputers successfully with exceptional children is addressed. This document features specific devices and models when referring to applications of calculators in the classroom. For the exceptional or handicapped student, calculators are viewed as the ''least restrictive'' learning device; they are destined to become more prominent in the classroom. The microcomputer is viewed as a device of the future, with great potential for adaptability. Currently available software functions and innovative devices, such as speech synthesizers, are noted. But no particular brands or models are described. The document concludes with a list of five ways calculators and/or computers can benefit students. The ways are: (1) reinforcing the basic skills; (2) helping in the basic skills of reasoning; (3) reinforcing problem-solving ability; (4) promoting logical thinking; and (5) encouraging creativity.

137. Computer-Based Instruction: A New Decade. Proceedings of the Annual Conference of the Association for the Development of Computer-Based Instructional Systems (Bellingham, Washington, March 31–April 3, 1980). Association for the Development of Computer-Based Instructional Systems, Apr 1980, 321p (ED 194 047; Reprint: EDRS).

The 50 papers in this collection from the 1980 ADCIS conference address topics ranging from coverage of large-scale CBE systems to specific single-purpose applications. Conference papers are presented in the following categories: Special Interest Group for the Handicapped; Mini-Micro Special Interest Group; Special Interest Group for Computer-Based Training; Elementary, Secondary, Junior College Special Interest Group; National Consortium for Computer-Based Music Instruction; Health Special Interest Group; National Consortium for CBE in Home Economics; Designing Instruction in the Basic Skills for Use with Micro Computer Technology; and PLATO Users Group. An author index is provided, and descriptions of 26 additional projects are attached.

138. Implications of MECC for B.C. School Computer Development. Discussion Paper 11/79. JEM Project No. 0610. Goddard, William P., British Columbia Department of Education, Victoria, BC, Canada. Information Service; JEM Research, Victoria, BC, Canada. Jun 1980, 18p (ED 208 844; Reprint EDRS).

This paper introduces a rationale and format for the introduction of microcomputers into British Columbia classrooms on a cost-effective basis. The three purposes of the paper are: (1) to briefly present the activities of the MECC; (2) to describe in general terms how British Columbia might benefit from the MECC experience through a particular adaptation to provincial needs; and (3) to encourage discussion among, and reaction from, the educational community. Descriptions of the background, operations, and specifications of MECC hardware and software are followed by suggestions for the development of a similar service in British Columbia.

The suggestions include a small-scale adaptation to meet 10 presently identified needs. The paper concludes with a request for reader reactions to add to JEM projects, information on the viability of the suggested JEM involvement, specification of school/district needs, identification of individuals who would be willing to share in the project, and identification of school districts which would consider first-stage involvement.

139. Leading a Child to a Computer Culture. AI Memo 343. Solomon, Cynthia J., Massachusetts Institute of Technology, Cambridge, MA. Artificial Intelligence Laboratory, Dec 4, 1975, 7p. Paper presented at SIGCSE-SIGCUE Symposium (Anaheim, CA, Feb 1976). Sponsoring Agency: National Institute of Education (DHEW), Washington, DC (ED 207 575; Reprint: EDRS).

This paper describes the way in which a child is introduced to LOGO, which is both a programing language and an environment or a way of thinking about computers and learning. After a brief description of the devices used by LOGO, the process of acquainting a student with the system is explained. The strong anthropomorphization of components of the LOGO system is discussed, with emphasis on the computer controlled mechanical turtles used in the system. Also discussed is the importance of having children learning to use LOGO to think of their projects as research enterprises. The 23 references listed include 11 working papers, memos, and reports on LOGO.

140. The Learner and the Computer. Ayers, George E. Oct 1980, 9p. Paper presented at the National Conference on Computer Based Education (Bloomington, MN, Oct 23–25, 1980) (ED 201 305; Reprint: EDRS).

The revolution in computers begun in the mid-1950s will help education meet the new challenges of the future generated by the predicted drastic declines in student enrollment and by changes in the types of learners served. Systems such as PLATO and TICCIT have proven that computers can provide useful and timely instruction for such learners as the disadvantaged, part-time adult student, the handicapped, and school dropouts—groups which will comprise a large segment of the educational population in the future. Computers can present instruction in developmental skills at a variety of levels, as well as more complex models of simulation, inquiry, and dialog. While the games industry has led in this direction, teachers themselves are now not only learning to program and develop courseware but are also initiating regional and national resource networks for sharing materials. The computer can also provide instruction for the handicapped through special input and output devices designed to increase their communication skills. Increased use of computers in the home, as well as for instructional purposes, will result in increased motivation for all learners, especially those young people who are potential high school dropouts.

141. Microcomputers in Education. Anderson, Cheryl A. Oct 1980, 13p (ED 198 812; Reprint: EDRS).

Designed to answer basic questions educators have about microcomputer hardware and software and their applications in teaching,

this paper describes the revolution in computer technology that has resulted from the development of the microchip processor. It provides information on the major computer components, i.e., input, central processing unit, memory, auxiliary storage, and output. The cost and time-saving advantages of a microcomputer purchase are discussed, as well as the instructional advantages. Various types of teaching strategies used with a computer are explained. The paper also includes a discussion of hardware selection criteria, software selection sources, and organizations which can provide the novice computer user with helpful information.

142. The Next Great Crisis in American Education: Computer Literacy. Molnar, Andrew R. Feb 1978, 17p. Based on comments made at the meeting of the Society for Applied Learning Technology (Orlando, FL, Feb 16, 1978). Contains occasional broken type. Sponsoring Agency: National Science Foundation, Washington, DC (ED 191 733; Reprint: EDRS).

Describes the current state of computer science education in this country. The information explosion in science and the shift in our economy, from the production of industrial goods to a greater emphasis on science and knowledge-based industries, has created a discontinuity in the nature of jobs and our educational needs. Computers are not a major part of American education but have become indispensable to the operation of science, business, and government. Many schools have introduced computers into their curriculum, but the paper stresses that these local efforts only partially satisfy the country's needs, at costs that are prohibitive and unnecessary when viewed nationally. Other nations have begun the task of restructuring their systems to include computers. It is stated that there is a national need to foster computer literacy, or the next crisis in American education will be the computer literacy crisis.

143. Proceedings of NECC/2 National Educational Computing Conference 1980 (Norfolk, Virginia, June 23–25, 1980). Harris, Diana, ed., Collison, Beth, ed., Iowa University, Iowa City, IA. Computer Center, Jun 1980, 306p (ED 194 060; Reprint: EDRS).

The record of these proceedings includes 52 papers and abstracts of 13 invited and nine tutorial sessions and provides an overview of the current status of computer usage in education and offers substantive forecasts for academic computing. Papers are presented under the following headings: "Business-Economics," "Tools and Techniques for Instruction," "Computers in Humanistic Studies," "Computer Literacy," "Science and Engineering," "Structured Programming," "ACM Elementary and Secondary Schools Subcommittee," "Computer Science Education," "Integrating Computing into K-12 Curriculum," "Mathematics, Testing-Placement," "Pre-College Instructional Materials," "Minority Institutions-ECMI," "Computer Laboratories in Education," "Computer Games in Instruction," and "Computing Curricula."

Abstracts are provided for 13 invited sessions dealing with such topics as: microcomputers in education; research in microcomputer uses; personal computing; educational computing: past, present and future; the Open University; CAUSE program and projects; funding academic computing programs; computer based resource sharing; computers and instruction; improving utilization of two-year college computer centers; teaching computer ethics; data sets available from the federal government; and MIS education, as well as nine tutorial sessions designed to provide attendees with the opportunity to expand their appreciation of and involvement in educational computing.

144. Using Computers to Enhance Teaching and Improve Teacher Centers. A Report of the National Teachers Centers Computer Technology Conference. Sadowski, Barbara R., ed.; Lovett, Charles, ed, Houston University, Houston, TX, 1981, 94p. Sponsoring Agency: Department of Education, Washington, DC (ED 205 478; Reprint: EDRS).

A conference of teacher center directors was held to explore the applications of computers to education. Three aspects of the conference were presented: management, information systems and communications, and instruction. The papers given at the conference provide a primer for teachers and teacher center directors who are beginning to work with computers. The first four papers give a perspective on the computer in society today and in the future, with illustrations of specific uses for computers in educational settings. Other papers discuss how teacher center communications and management can be improved through the use of microcomputers and how computer assisted or computer managed instruction can be used in schools. Positive implications for teachers are also presented. Appendices provide a glossary and list educational computer resources and organizations.

BOOKS

145. The Computer in the School: Tutor, Tool, Tutee. Taylor, Robert, ed. Totowa, NJ: Teachers College Press, 1980, 274p.

Nineteen essays by five pioneers in the field of computers in education are presented in this volume. The essays provide a foundation for understanding the basic issues involved in using computers in schools, the teacher's role in helping the student make full use of computing, and the general limitations of computer use. A framework is presented for considering computers in education, which identifies three functions of a computer: as a tutor, as a tool, or as a student (tutee). A computer's tutor function requires expert programing so that flexible computer assisted instruction can be provided to students. A computer's tool function requires only that some useful capability (such as statistical analysis) be programed into the computer. In the student or tutee function of a computer, a human tutor teaches the computer, thereby enhancing human learning and reducing software costs. Other topics of discussion include interactive learning, heuristic strategies, pre- and postcollege computer education, ways to teach children to think, mathematics education, the future of computers in education, and teachers and computer assisted instruction.

146. Mindstorms; Children, Computers and Powerful Ideas. Papert, Seymour. New York, NY: Basic Books, Inc., Publishers, 1980, 230p.

This book shows how fundamental concepts of mathematics can be understood and mastered by young children by providing a learning environment in which children are communicating with computers in a natural and easy way. Presents ways computers can be carriers of powerful ideas that cut across the traditional lines separating the humanities from the sciences. Much of the book is devoted to building up images of the computer's role that are very different from current stereotypes.

147. The Social Impact of Computers. Silver, Gerald A. New York: Harcourt Brace Jovanovich, Inc., 1979, 342p.

Presents an analysis, not only of the mechanical aspects of computers, but also of how computers are now used and may be used in the future and how their use affects society. Also explores the legal, ethical, economic, and psychological questions surrounding the increasing use of computers.

Classroom Applications

"Classroom Applications" has been defined very broadly in this section. Games, activities, lesson plans, and simulations all fall into this category. "Classroom Applications" is used mainly to differentiate what takes place in the classroom from what takes place in an administrative situation (Management Applications). There is, however, some overlap with the "Management Applications" section, especially when a document discusses the myriad capabilities and potentials of microcomputers, including both classroom and management applications.

There is also some overlap with the "Computer Literacy" section, such as when a document addresses an approach to computer literacy itself, though the focus of the "Computer Literacy" section is on what computer literacy is, how an entire school, district, or state becomes computer literate, or on various definitions of computer literacy itself. If the document at hand seemed to contain enough information on goals or objectives or scope and sequence of a computer literacy program to actually implement the program, it was placed in this "Classroom Applications" section.

Included in this section are documents which discuss specific computer languages (LOGO and BASIC mostly), how to integrate computers into the classroom, how to use microcomputers in specific subject areas (mathematics and reading mostly), and how to get more mileage out of micros through the use of travelling teachers or vans which serve a whole district.

Often, in this section, sample lessons are included. Guides which include course objectives or scope and sequence skills, methods for identifying students with an aptitude for programing, and descriptions of microcomputer centers which have been set up in the classroom or resource center are also covered.

JOURNAL ARTICLES

148. **ACM ES³ Preliminary Report on Computer Science Curriculum.** Rogers, Jean. *The Computing Teacher.* v7, n5, p12–16, Apr–May 1980.

   This report makes a number of recommendations for a one-year, secondary school computer science course, including possible course content, suggestions for facilities and resources, and ways of integrating the course into the existing school program.

149. **Acting Out the Computer.** Beyer, Kathleen. *The Computing Teacher.* v6, n4, p13–14, May 1979.

   A description is given of a supplemental unit for a primary-level computer literacy class in which a play is produced with all students taking roles as parts of a computer.

150. **Action Research Roundup.** Stein, Gloria, et al. *Classroom Computer News.* v2, n2, p18–20, Nov–Dec 1981.

   Reports on three studies of microcomputer based learning: (1) the teaching of problem-solving skills in grades K-9; (2) the effects of access to microcomputers on the math achievement of high-achieving fifth- and sixth-grade students; and (3) the effect of daily drill and practice on the math achievement of third- and fourth-grade students.

151. **Adam Comes to Nueva.** Laycock, Mary. *Arithmetic Teacher.* v27, n5, p46–47, Jan 1980 (EJ 216 651; Reprint: UMI).

   The results of the interaction of fifth- and sixth-grade students with a computer are described.

152. **The Algorithm Model for Schooling: An "All Win" Combination.** Levy, Phyllis Saltzman. *NASSP Bulletin.* v65, n443, p54–60, Mar 1981.

   Presents a plan whereby all teachers and all students could become computer literate. A sample lesson series is included.

153. **BASIC Programming for Gifted Elementary Students.** Wiebe, James H. *Arithmetic Teacher.* v28, n7, p42–44, Mar 1981 (EJ 242 910; Reprint: UMI).

   The instruction of BASIC programing to gifted and other interested pupils from grades 5–8 in Tempe, Arizona is described. Sample assignments and major recommendations for people planning to begin BASIC programing courses for elementary students are featured.

154. **A Case and Techniques for Computers: Using Computers in Middle School Mathematics.** Hatfield, Larry L. *Arithmetic Teacher.* v26, n6, p53–55, Feb 1979 (EJ 198 503; Reprint: UMI).

   Potential uses for computers include: programing the solutions to problems; simulating situations in order to test hypotheses; gaming, as a study of probability and statistics; and practicing, testing, and tutoring.

155. Case Studies in Computerism. Eisenrich, Jane. *Educational Computer Magazine*. v2, n1, p36–37, Jan–Feb 1982 (Available from P.O. Box 535, Cupertino, CA)

The author presents entertaining profiles of young (upper elementary) computer learner types and includes a checklist for rating potential computer programers.

156. Come in and Play with Me: Computer Simulations: A Key to Divergent Thinking. Steffin, Sherwin A. *Media and Methods*. v18, n2, p12–13, Oct 1981.

Argues that computer simulations are an excellent way to promote student's divergent thinking skills because they include firm criteria for acceptable solutions, strong positive reinforcement, immediate feedback, and infinite patience to allow the learner to experiment with ideas.

157. Compu-Kids: A Project for "Children" of All Ages. Statz, Joyce A. *Arithmetic Teacher*. v25, n8, p48–50, May 1978 (EJ 185 553; Reprint: UMI).

An after-school program in which fifth and sixth graders were taught how to use the BASIC programing language with computer terminals is described.

158. Computer Animation Helps Children to Learn. Bryan, Sam D. *onComputing*. v2, n1, p18–19, Sum 1980 (EJ 226 854; Reprint: UMI).

Described is an animated computer program designed to help the young child match lower-case and upper-case letters. The Intecolor 8052 personal computer made by Intelligent Systems Corporation (SC) was used, but the program could also be written for the Radio Shack TRS-80, PET, Apple, Atari, and ISCs Compucolor II.

159. Computer-Assisted Instruction Is Not Always Drill. Hutcheson, James W. *Mathematics Teacher*. v73, n9, p689–92, Dec 1980 (EJ 237 485; Reprint: UMI).

Use of computer programs as tools for instruction on statistics is presented. A program for TRS-80 Level II BASIC is included.

160. Computer Countdown. Hansen, Chris. *Creative Computing*. v6, n9, p98, Sep 1980.

Describes how one middle school created a small microcomputer room with three PETs and promoted student interest by giving the room an outer space theme.

161. Computer Curriculum: Scope and Sequence. Fawson, Paul C. *The Computing Teacher*. v8, n2, p48–49, 1980–81.

Presents a scope and sequence of skills necessary to develop staff and student proficiency in computer use. Suggestions are divided into three levels: elementary, junior high school, and high school.

162. Computer Game Playing—"Turn On" to Mathematics. Winner, Alice-Ann; McClung, Margo D. *Arithmetic Teacher*. v29, n2, p38–39, Oct 1981 (EJ 252 786; Reprint: UMI).

The success pupils experience with the computer allows them to attempt mastery of skills previously rejected and to attempt understanding of concepts previously thought too difficult.

163. Computer Games in the Classroom. Fisher, Glenn. *Recreational Computing*. v9, n4, p52–53, Jan 1981.

The author discusses the educational uses of arcade games, logic (including board and card) games, tutorials, and simulations.

164. The Computer Goes to Nursery School. Swigger, Kathleen; Campbell, James. *Educational Computer Magazine*. v1, n2, p10–12, Jul–Aug 1981.

How early is early enough? At North Texas State University Nursery School, preschoolers are learning basic skills and concepts with the help of computers.

165. Computer Pioneer. Potts, Michael. *Instructor*. v90, n10, p74–75, May 1981 (EJ 243 450; Reprint: UMI).

The author describes how he has integrated a TRS-80 microcomputer into his second-grade classroom as a tutor, an enrichment resource, and a record keeping tool. He outlines some of the benefits this microcomputer has brought to his students and himself.

166. Computers and Kids: A New Center Offers Children Hands On Experience. Holmes, Edith. *Bulletin of the American Society for Information Science*. v7, n5, p12–16, Jun 1981 (EJ 252 527; Reprint: UMI).

Discusses computer programs and courses offered to children and teachers at the new Future Center at the Capitol Children's Museum. Describes the displays and activities of the communications exhibit and Kid-Net, a minicomputer based time-sharing system for which a series of computer programs for visitor use will be developed.

167. Computers and Middle School Mathematics. Henry, Loren L. *Viewpoints in Teaching and Learning*. v57, n2, p46–54, Spr 1981 (EJ 247 948; Reprint: UMI).

Potential instructional uses of the computer for expanding middle-school mathematics programs are described. Content areas which are represented include geometry, number theory, computation, consumer education, and probability.

168. Computers. . . . Are All Dinosaurs Dead? Glover, Douglas. *G/C/T*. v1, n4, p16–17, 46–50, Sep–Oct 1978 (EJ 206 376; Reprint: UMI).

The article describes the University of Southern Alabama's Saturday Program for Gifted Children (8-18 years old), which uses TRS-80 microcomputers. With the computers, the children not only gain background knowledge about a particular area, but learn computer programing as well.

169. Computers Are Their Thing. Jones, Aubrey B., Jr. *Technological Horizons in Education*. v8, n1, p54–56, 61, Jan 1981 (EJ 252 815; Reprint: UMI).

Describes a pilot project in Philadelphia which introduced seventh- and eighth-grade minority students to computers as a means of building their self-confidence and encouraging them to pursue careers in engineering and computer science. Includes partial course outline, evaluation methods, and tips for success.

170. Computers at an Alternative School. Stone, Deborah. *Creative Computing*. v6, n9, p46–47, Sep 1980.

The author, from a tiny private tutorial school (grades 3–12), describes how the school acquired two microcomputers and introduced them to the students. The machines are not formally integrated into the curriculum, rather, students teach themselves and use the computers to play games and write programs.

171. Computers in Reading: A Review of Applications and Implications. Thompson, Barbara J. *Educational Technology*. v20, n8, p38–41, Aug 1980 (EJ 232 552; Reprint: UMI).

Briefly summarizes the applications and implications of computer assisted instruction, computer managed instruction, and computer based resource units. Other computer applications and research are discussed.

172. Computers in the Kindergarten. Hungate, Harriet. *The Computing Teacher*. v9, n5, p15–18, Jan 1982.

Kindergarten children at a San Francisco Bay area school had weekly contact with Commodore PET microcomputers from October 1980 through May 1981 so that computer programs could be developed that would systematically teach certain skills. This paper describes the children's reactions and the sequence of programs used.

173. Computing at a New Public School for Gifted Students. Davis, Steve; Frothingham, Phyllis S. *onComputing*. v2, n4, p72–75, Spr 1981 (EJ 239 746; Reprint: UMI).

At the North Carolina School of Science and Mathematics, microcomputers and minicomputers are being integrated into all aspects of the high school program. This report describes the rationale behind and some of the features of the school's computer program.

174. Computing in an Elementary School. Winner, Alice-Ann. *The Computing Teacher*. v7, n6, p26–27, Jun–Jul 1980.

Describes how two TRS-80 microcomputers are being used by upper elementary students and their teachers in a private school.

175. Cooperation and Computing. Isenberg, Robert. *Classroom Computer News*. v2, n2, p24–25, Nov–Dec 1981.

Describes how computers can improve students' interpersonal skills through group work on simulations.

176. Cupertino School District Develops Computer Literacy Curriculum. *The Computing Teacher*. v9, n1, p27–34, Sep 1981.

Presents the scope and sequenced objectives of this California district's K-8 computer literacy curriculum. Objectives and activities, to be provided in social studies, language arts, science and mathematics, or in a single computer literacy elective, are delineated for the following grade levels: K-3, 4-6, and 7-8.

177. A Dozen Apples for the Classroom. Hakansson, Joyce; Roach, Leslie. *Creative Computing*. v5, n9, p52–54, Sep 1979 (EJ 210 094; Reprint: UMI).

A description is given of the Science Shuttle program, which uses a van to bring Apple II into the classroom.

178. An '80 in the Apple. Radin, Stephen. *80 Microcomputing*. n26, p68–69, Feb 1982.

An inner-city junior high school teacher explains how his school acquired microcomputers and is making use of them. Both students and teachers are involved in writing CAI programs for basic skills instruction.

179. Elementary Problem-Solving with the Microcomputer. Winner, Alice-Ann. *The Computing Teacher*. v9, n6, p11–14, Feb 1982.

Suggests ways elementary school teachers can incorporate the microcomputer into the classroom by using the natural interests of young children.

180. Elementary School Computer-Related Activities. Moursund, David. *The Computing Teacher*. v7, n5, p28–31, Apr–May 1980.

Addressed to elementary teachers, this article suggests a variety of activities for increasing children's awareness and knowledge of computers, using a microcomputer, calculators, or no equipment at all.

181. Explaining Computer Related Concepts & Terminology. Lawson, Harold W., Jr. *Creative Computing*. v7, n10, p92, 94, 96–100, 102, Oct 1981 (EJ 252 713; Reprint: UMI).

A process-oriented approach that can be highly successful in introducing students to computer systems concepts and terminology in an integrated manner is presented.

182. 5th, 6th Graders Practice Logic and Program on High School and College Level. Robertson, Nancy. *80 Microcomputing*. n14, p52–53, Feb 1981.

This article describes the computer education program at Cumberland Elementary School. The program's success is documented with test scores showing gains in problem-solving and computation skills and with the story of five of its star pupils who went from Cumberland directly to an accelerated computer language course in Pascal at Purdue University.

183. The First "R": Reading Practice with the TRS-80 Voice Synthesizer. Rogers, John F. *Creative Computing*. v6, n4, p62, Apr 1980 (EJ 222 471; Reprint: UMI).

The development of a voice synthesizer gives a microcomputer the ability to speak and thus drill a student in reading. A computer program is included.

184. For the New Computing Teacher: Some Notes on Getting Started. Stein, Gloria. *Classroom Computer News*. v2, n3, p21–22, 56, Jan–Feb 1982.

Intended for the elementary teacher who has just acquired a microcomputer for the classroom, this article presents tips on placement of the machine in the room, planning a schedule for student use, and selecting quality software packages with which to get started.

185. Goals for Computer Education. *Calculators/Computers Magazine.* v2, n7, p23–25, Nov–Dec 1978.

This list of goals, program objectives, and instructional objectives for grades K-12 is keyed according to type of competency, type of learning, and grade level.

186. Have Computer—Will Travel. Richman, Ellen. *Creative Computing.* v5, n9, p56–57, Sep 1979 (EJ 210 095; Reprint: UMI).

A description of a course for grades 4-8 using the Apple II microcomputer is given.

187. Ideas. Tabler, M. Bernadine; Jacobson, Marilyn Hall. *Arithmetic Teacher.* v28, n9, p19-24, May 1981 (EJ 246 312; Reprint: UMI).

Provides worksheets and teaching ideas that focus on reading data generated by a computer; input media with emphasis on one type of punched card; flowcharting; and simple program-writing to solve word problems. Grade levels are primarily 5-8.

188. The Integration of Microcomputers into the Classroom or Now That I've Got It, What Do I Do with It? Keyser, Earl L. *AEDS Journal.* v13, n1, p113–17, Fall 1979. (EJ 223 577; Reprint: UMI).

Provides a few examples of how microcomputers are used in the classroom, emphasizing the advantages of the small machine. Notes the availability of tools to create instructional materials on the microcomputer.

189. Interfacing an Inexpensive Home Computer to the Videodisc: Educational Applications for the Hearing Impaired. Galbraith, Gary, et al. *American Annals of the Deaf (Educational Technology for the '80's).* v124, n5, p536–41, Sep 1979 (EJ 216 200; Reprint: UMI).

Originally part of a symposium on educational media for the deaf, the article describes the use of computer assisted instruction to teach young deaf and multiply handicapped children. The microcomputer/videodisc interface is explained, and the method of captioning the videodisc is discussed. Diagrams illustrate the process.

190. Introducing Computers in the Elementary School. Lynch, Charlotte. *The Computing Teacher.* v8, n2, p5–7, 1980–81.

This article is part of a practicum course report detailing the design and implementation of a course for sixth-grade students.

191. Introducing Microcomputers to Instructional Education. Bjorum, William. *The Computing Teacher.* v8, n5, p39–40, 1980-81.

Describes the organized start-up efforts of Independent School District 834, Stillwater, Minnesota, once they decided to take advantage of the microcomputer.

192. An Introduction to Computers and Computing: A High School Course Outline. Rogers, Jean B. *The Computing Teacher.* v8, n7, p30–33, 1980-81.

Provides an outline of topics that might be covered in a general course for every student at the high school level.

193. It's Not All Drill and Practice. Klitzer, Carol. *Personal Computing.* v5, n4, Apr 1981.

The author looks briefly at two types of educational software. With the first type, which includes drill-and-practice and tutorials, the computer instructs the student. The second genre of software, exemplified by the LOGO language and simulations, allows the student to control the computer and use it as a tool for problem solving.

194. Kids and Computers: The Future Is Today. Larsen, Sally Greenwood. *Creative Computing.* v5, n9, p58–60, Sep 1979 (EJ 210 096; Reprint: UMI).

Examples are given of the way computers are introduced to gifted third and fourth graders in Racine, Wisconsin elementary schools.

195. Kids Compute the Darndest Things. Moskowitz, Robert. *InfoWorld.* v3, n4, p43–44, Jul 20 1981.

A look at some young computer whiz kids, ages 5 to 20.

196. Learning with Logo. Nelson, Harold. *onComputing.* v3, n1, p14–16, Sum 1981 (EJ 245 098; Reprint: UMI).

Describes a new computer language called LOGO and the use of personal computers with very young children at Dallas' Lamplighter school, where computers are everywhere—one in each preschool and kindergarten room, two in each elementary classroom; and two in each shared space.

197. Let the Young Einstein Shine. Hollifield, John. *Educational R & D Report.* v5, n1, p2–6, Spr 1980.

Describes two computer simulated physics experiments which let students use the scientific method to learn physics concepts and processes.

198. LOGO: A Learning Environment for Learning-Disabled Students. Weir, Sylvia; Watt, Daniel. *The Computing Teacher.* v8, n5, p11–19, 1980–81.

This paper describes a project designed to provide an innovative computer based learning environment for learning disabled students in grades 5-8.

199. A Microcomputer Minicurriculum. Feeney, John E. *The Arithmetic Teacher.* v29, n5, p39–42, Jan 1982.

Presents 10 activity cards designed to introduce upper-elementary students to the elements of programing BASIC through mathematics.

200. Microcomputers for Gifted Microtots. Doorly, Ann. *G/C/T.* n14, p62–64, Sep–Oct 1980 (EJ 236 760; Reprint: UMI).

The use of microcomputers for mathematically gifted primary-grade children is examined. Class activities include discussion of the development and types of computers, basic number operations, and actual programing.

201. Microcomputers in Special Schools. Hart, Bob; Staples, Ian. *Special Education: Forward Trends.* v7, n4, p22–25, Dec 1980 (EJ 240 543; Reprint: UMI).

The author considers the value of microcomputers as a link between research and classroom teaching styles and describes programs in which microcomputers are used with handicapped children.

202. Micros "GOTO" School. Piele, Donald T. *Creative Computing.* v5, n9, p132–34, Sep 1979 (EJ 210 101; Reprint: UMI).

This article reports on a pilot project in which an Apple II microcomputer was placed in a sixth-grade classroom for six weeks with the purpose of developing logical thinking skills through programing instruction. Sample lessons are included, and the enthusiastic reaction of students—both boys and girls—is noted.

203. My Computer Likes Me. Firedrake, George; Zamora, Ramon. *Popular Computing.* v1, n1, p58, 60, 62, 64, 66, Nov 1981.

Presents a lesson plan for showing children how to operate a TRS-80 Color Computer.

204. My TRS-80 Likes Me. Albrecht, Bob. *Calculators/Computers Magazine.* v2, n6, p9–11, Sep–Oct 1978.

Presents some ideas on helping students learn how to understand simple programs in TRS-80 BASIC.

205. My TRS-80 Likes Me. Part 2. Albrecht, Bob. *Calculators/Computers Magazine.* v2, n7, p63–64, Nov–Dec 1978.

Random number generation by computers is discussed. A BASIC program is given that uses random numbers to print a given name in random positions at given time intervals.

206. PET BASIC for Parents and Teachers. Albrecht, Bob; Albrecht, Karl. *Calculators/Computers Magazine.* v2, n7, p46–47, Nov–Dec 1978.

A notation is suggested to make listings of Commodore PET programs more readable by parents and teachers. Some samples are given.

207. PETS for Little People. Alper, Lynne. *The Computing Teacher.* v8, n7, p54–55, 1980–81.

Describes how Cragmont School in Berkeley, California has introduced computers into its K-3 curriculum through games that develop students' mathematical, verbal, and problem-solving skills. Suggests some guidelines for encouraging computer use in a school.

208. Playing Computer—A Computer Literacy Activity for the Elementary Grades. Feddern, Barbara. *The Computing Teacher.* v9, n2, p57–59, Oct 1981.

Outlines an activity for grades 2-6 in which students act out, step by step, the way a computer solves a problem. The one prop

needed is the memory board, whose simple construction is explained.

209. Playing for Space—Two Classroom Games. Mandell, Alan; Kannan, Madeline. *Science Teacher.* v48, n6, p22–23, Sep 1981 (EJ 252 700; Reprint: UMI).

Describes two games which may be used with pairs or teams of students in earth/space science courses to reinforce and enrich content and to review subject matter. A microcomputer program written in BASIC II is provided.

210. Programs for Small Children. Lucas, Jay P. *Creative Computing.* v6, n3, p136–37, Mar 1980.

This article presents three program listings written in ALTAIR Disk BASIC 4.0 for toddlers. They were constructed to protect the computer, as well as to enlighten the young child. The first program simply generates a response when the child touches the keys. The other two programs are for simple character and shape recognition.

211. A Short Presentation in "Computer Literacy" Using Programmable Calculators. Wayrik, John J. *Calculators/Computers Magazine.* v2, n7, p9–11, Nov–Dec 1978.

The programmable calculator is suggested as a means of introducing elementary school students to certain features of computers. A one-hour presentation is described.

212. Teaching First Graders How a Computer Can Sort. Hedges, William D. *The Computing Teacher.* v8, n5, p24–25, 1980–81.

Demonstrates how children can grasp some very powerful computer concepts if imaginative teaching methods are employed.

213. Teaching Fourth and Fifth Graders about Computers. Zukas, Walter X., et al. *Arithmetic Teacher.* v28, n2, p24–27, Oct 1980 (EJ 232 915; Reprint: UMI).

Tells about a minicourse, designed to teach fourth and fifth graders about computers, that includes decoding computer cards, a "race" against the computer, a field trip, flow charting, and writing computer programs.

214. The TRS-80 as a Classroom Teaching Tool. Spero, Samuel W. *Calculators/Computers Magazine.* v2, n7, p58–59, Nov–Dec 1978.

The use of the computer as an aid to the classroom teacher is discussed. A list is given of projects developed for classroom use in the areas of mathematics, science, social studies, and English.

215. Two Programs from a Young Eighth-Grader. Bahcall, Safi; Nelson, Harold. *onComputing.* v2, n3, p38–42, Win 1980 (EJ 233 503; Reprint: UMI).

To illustrate what a young, self-taught computer enthusiast can accomplish, 11-year-old Safi Bahcall presents two BASIC computer programs he developed. The first converts numbers from one mathematical base to another. The second monitors commodity investments. In his introduction, Harold Nelson notes some of Safi's other computer achievements.

216. Using an Information Retrieval System in Junior High Schools. Nerby, Connie; Hilgenfield, Bob. *The Computing Teacher.* v9, n1, p53–54, Sep 1981.

Describes a junior high school program where students learn to use ''The Source'' information retrieval network.

MICROFICHE

217. Computer Applications in Reading. Mason, George E.; Blanchard, Jay S., International Reading Association, Newark, DE, 1979, 115p (ED 173 771; Reprint: EDRS; also available from International Reading Association, 800 Barkdale Road, Newark, DE 19711).

Constituting the first full treatment of computers in reading, this volume focuses on recent developments in computer assisted instruction and its classroom implications. The eight chapters provide information on the following topics: development of digital computers and of programs for using them for educational purposes, development of computer based reading programs by college centers, public school applications of computers to reading instruction, computer assessment of readability and textbook analysis, sources of computer services, recommended uses of computers in the reading program, computers in reading research, and the future of the computer as an aid to reading instruction. Extensive annotated references are provided for each chapter.

218. Computer Education Guide. Newark School District, DE, Aug 1976, 64p (ED 158 729; Reprint: EDRS).

Recognizing the need for all students to be aware of the nature and functions of the computer in modern society, as well as to be computer literate in specific major fields, this guide was developed to aid secondary school teachers determine how to integrate computer education in their courses. The first of the five goals presented addresses the general need for awareness by all students; remaining goals are concerned with both awareness of and involvement in computer applications in specific areas—the business field for all business students, the academic subject areas for all college-bound students, and more specialized applications for social-science-oriented and science- and mathematics-oriented college-bound students. Educational and specific instructional objectives, suggested activities, strategies, topics, and notes are provided for each goal. A flow chart is included for determining which goals are applicable in specific courses. Appendices include lists of films and simulation activities relevant to specific academic areas, which could be used to help meet these goals and objectives.

219. Computer Simulation and Its Instructional Uses. The Illinois Series on Educational Application of Computers, No. 8e. Dennis, J. Richard, Illinois University, Urbana, IL. Department of Secondary Education, 1979, 34p. Sponsoring Agency: EXXON Education Foundation, New York, NY (ED 183 188; Reprint: EDRS).

This paper discusses computer simulation as a tool for teaching about phenomena characterized by a problem to be solved, a task or goal to be reached, a procedure to be learned, or an environment to be understood. Simulation is defined and characterized by an examination of both the attributes that are common to simulations and a taxonomy (classification) of simulations based upon attributes not common to all instances of simulation. The many aspects of using simulations in the classroom are also discussed. This document was prepared as a resource for the preservice and inservice training of teachers, and it points out that, although simulations can be a valuable teaching tool, in order to use them effectively, teachers need to be aware of their nature, what learning experiences they can potentially provide, and the provisions that must be made to optimize their use. A list of sources of existing simulations and a 27-item bibliography are attached.

220. Fractions Curriculum of the PLATO Elementary School Mathematics Project. 2nd Edition. Dugdale, Sharon; Kibbey, David, Illinois University, Urbana, IL. Computer-Based Education Research Laboratory, Jul 1980, 159p. Sponsoring Agency: National Science Foundation, Washington, DC (ED 201 322; Reprint: EDRS).

Designed to provide intermediate-grade students with experience using fractions and mixed numbers, the PLATO computer system sequence described in this manual includes interactive models for students to work with, as well as lessons for review, practice, or experience. These lessons are intended to be integrated with the classroom mathematics instruction, and introductory materials describe the implementation of the lessons, student assignments, the student session, data feedback to teachers, and supplementary materials. The development of the curriculum and results of external evaluation studies are also briefly reviewed. The descriptions of 16 selected modules that make up the bulk of the manual include a statement of purpose, brief description, and sample computer displays for each lesson.

Topics covered include the meanings, ordering and equivalence, conversions, addition, subtraction, and multiplication of fractions and mixed numbers, as well as the meanings of decimal fractions and conversions to or from fractions whose denominator is a power of 10. Appendices include samples of student responses in creative activities shared with other students, a brief review of some other uses of the PLATO fractions materials, simplified flow charts illustrating the instructional modules, a list of related publications, and an index to the lesson descriptions by title.

221. Microcomputers ''Goto'' School. Piele, Donald T. Apr 1979, 13p. Paper presented at the Annual Meeting of the American Educational Research Association (San Francisco, CA, Apr 12, 1979) (ED 172 776; Reprint: EDRS).

This paper is a report of a pilot project in which a microcomputer was placed in a sixth-grade classroom for eight weeks with the purpose of developing logical thinking skills. Students were first taught how to program the Apple II microcomputer to draw color graphics designs. They were then given similar problems to solve, using the commands they had learned. Sample programs are included, as well as student responses to a questionnaire, which were highly positive.

222. Teacher's Guide for Computational Models of Animal Behavior: A Computer-Based Curriculum Unit to Accompany the Elementary Science Study Guide ''Behavior of Mealworms.'' Artificial Intelligence Memo No. 432. Abelson, Hal; Goldenberg, Paul, Massachusetts Institute of Technology, Cambridge, MA. Artificial Intelligence Laboratory, Apr 1977,

35p. Sponsoring Agency: National Science Foundation, Washington, DC (ED 207 798; Reprint: EDRS; also available from Artificial Intelligence Laboratory, 545 Technology Square, Room 338, Cambridge, MA 02139).

This experimental curriculum unit suggests how dramatic innovations in classroom content may be achieved through the use of computers. The computational perspective is viewed as one which can enrich and transform traditional curricula, act as a focus for integrating insights from diverse disciplines, and enable learning to become more active- and project-oriented. This unit suggests how an interplay of computer and noncomputer activities could occur with elementary school biology. This material is envisioned as a second exposure to the LOGO programing language. Hence, the issues of introducing students to the basics of writing procedures and controlling turtles are not discussed. The focus is on illustrating how accessible computer oriented facilities can be integrated into the classroom environment. The unit is prepared as a companion to the Elementary School Science Study's *Teacher's Guide to Behavior of Mealworms*.

223. The Use of the Portable Computer in Classroom Instruction. McTeer, J. Hugh; Jackson, Barry N. 1978, 8p (ED 186 339; Reprint: EDRS).

This paper describes a computer assisted instruction program which was used in a senior high school local government course. In the fall of 1978, a contract was worked out with four senior American government students who were also studying fifth-year mathematics. In return for writing a computer program on local government, which would count as 25 percent of the second nine weeks' grade in both classes, the students were given some release time from regular classroom activities in both the government and the mathematics classes. Some homework was also eliminated for these students. The program was written in basic computer language for a TRS-80 Radio Shack Level II computer. The particular data statements were designed to question students on local county government. The computer logic, however, could be used in any other subject area, and the teacher would only have to develop different data statements to fit the different subject areas.

The data for the local government course consisted of 99 questions—33 questions each of multiple choice, true or false, and fill in the blank. The program was used in various ways. For example, individual students used the computer for remedial work. The program has also been used as a pretest of the student's knowledge of local government. The program provides direct feedback, since incorrect responses are immediately noted; students are given correct answers; and students are given page numbers in the textbook when they need extra help and information. The program has increased student interest in the course.

Management Applications

This section is designed to provide some background on the use of microcomputers for routine administrative tasks. Included are documents which address some of the areas where micros might be used most profitably: (1) word processing; (2) school attendance records; (3) student records; (4) test scoring; (5) budgeting; (6) payroll/personnel records; (7) data storage; (8) program evaluation; (9) readability level calculations of written materials; (10) student immunization records; and (12) student scheduling. There is also a fairly heavy representation of documents which deal with the uses of micros in the library. Computer Assisted Instruction programs and Computer Managed Instruction programs also fall into this section.

There is some overlap between this section and the "Classroom Applications" section, especially for documents which discuss the multiple capabilities of micros in general. There is also some overlap with the "Selection/Evaluation" section where documents discuss selecting and evaluating hardware and software for administrative purposes.

In all cases, an attempt was made to place the document into the appropriate section, based on emphasis and focus of the document. However, use of the index will help to pinpoint documents of most value to the reader.

JOURNAL ARTICLES

224. Administrative Decision Tools—A Microcomputer Reality Available Now. Judd, Dorothy H. *Educational Computer Magazine*. v1, n2, p6–7, Jul–Aug 1982 (Available from P.O. Box 535, Cupertino; CA 95015.

Reviews some existing administrative software packages, including six packages prepared in Applesoft Basic by the Northwest Regional Educational Laboratory of Portland, Oregon.

225. An Apple a Day: Microcomputers in the Public Library. Romans, Anne F.; Ransom, Stanley A. *American Libraries*. v11, n11, p692–93, Dec 1980 (EJ 239 059; Reprint: UMI).

Describes a program at the Plattsburgh Public Library in upstate New York designed to bring basic computer literacy to rural children. The program utilizes an Apple II Plus system and focuses on two aspects of computer literacy: software use and programing.

226. Avoid Readability Formula Drudgery: Use Your School's Microcomputer. Judd, Dorothy H. *Reading Teacher*. v35, n1, p7–8, Oct 1981. (EJ 252 111; Reprint: UMI).

Argues that the use of microcomputers and prewritten computer programs can save teachers time and effort in calculating the readability levels of written materials.

227. CAM Challenges Students to Perform Better. Ryan, Suzanne K. *Educational Leadership*. v37, n7, p590–93, Apr 1980.

Describes a unique educational monitoring and achievement program: Comprehensive Achievement Monitoring.

228. Can the Microcomputer Assist in Data Base Management? Judd, Robert C. *Educational Computer Magazine*. v2, n1, p20–22, Jan–Feb 1982 (Available from P.O. Box 535, Cuppertino, CA 95015).

Guidelines for the school principal on implementing school-level records programs are presented. Hardware requirements are discussed, and specific software packages for each popular microcomputer brand are suggested.

229. Classrooms Make Friends with Computers. Spivak, Howard; Varden, Stuart. *Instructor*. v89, n8, p84–86, Mar 1980 (EJ 220 471; Reprint: UMI).

The authors cite specific ways that the classroom computer can aid the teacher: by providing a wide variety of independent instruction for students and by cutting down the time required for record keeping, testing, and other administrative tasks.

230. The Computer as an Instructional Medium. Peray, Tom; Keyser, Ed. *Clearing House*. v53, n4, p172–74, Dec 1979.

Presents the many uses of computers in education, along with a brief discussion of several specific programs.

231. A Computer First for an Elementary School: Microcomputer Replaces Card Catalog. Malsam, Margaret. *Educational Computer Magazine*. v1, n3, p40–41, 53, Sep–Oct 1981.

Describes the use of a microcomputer in an elementary school library. It may be the first library in the nation to have all of its books listed on computers, rather than filed in the traditional card catalog.

232. Computer Managed Instruction. Allen, Michael. *Journal of Research and Development in Education*. v14, n1, p33–640, Fall 1980.

Computer Managed Instruction (CMI) and Computer Assisted Instruction (CAI) are defined, and the components and capabilities of CMI are discussed.

233. Computer Revolution in the Learning Resources Center. Daehler, Russ; Kuszynski, Larry. *Technological Horizons in Education*. v7, n4, p34–35, May 1980.

Automating a library system via computer can increase efficient handling of all operations, including circulation, cataloging, acquisition, and bibliographic reference.

234. Computers Can Manage, and Assist with, Instruction. Bozeman, William C., Thomas, David B. *Executive Educator*. v2, n3, p23–25, Mar 1980.

Presents the challenges facing central office administrators: a scarcity of good computer people, good software, and incompatible computer languages.

235. Computers Help Students Get Shot. *Personal Computing*. v6, n2, p98, 100, Feb 1982.

West Side High School in New York City has developed a database system using Commodore computers to handle student immunization records.

236. Computers in the Schools: Now that We Have Them . . . ? Eisele, James E. *Educational Technology*. v21, n10, p24–27, Oct 1981.

This article deals with some directions that microcomputer technology uniquely suited to education should move in: (1) development of comprehensive instructional systems; (2) development of advanced instructional strategies; (3) promotion of universal computer literacy; and (4) use of microcomputers to teach problem-solving skills.

237. Facilities for Microcomputers. Lopez, Antonio M., Jr. *American School and University*. v54, n4, p34–35, 38, 40, Dec 1981.

Discusses the facility requirements for microcomputers, both in the school office and in the academic program, for computer assisted instruction. Briefly describes the microcomputer learning laboratories in three New Orleans high schools.

238. Hardware and Software: Directory of Manufacturers. *American School and University*. v54, n4, p26–28, Dec 1981.

This annotated directory emphasizes sources of software for educational administration.

239. How Many Ways Can the Computer Be Used in Education? A Baker's Dozen. Roecks, Alan L. *Educational Technology*. v21, n9, p16, Sep 1981.

Responding to Alan Watts (*Educational Technology*, April 1981, pages 18–22), who found 12 uses for computers in education, the author reports from his survey findings a 13th use: institutional coordination.

240. How to Determine the Strategic Potential of Computer-Based Instruction in Your Training/Education Department. Svenson, Raynold A. *Technological Horizons in Education*. v8, n3, p36–38, 42 Mar 1981 (EJ 252 823; Reprint: UMI).

Outlines a study procedure for directors, administrators, and managers of large-scale training or education functions to determine if computer based instruction is cost-effective for their organization. Plan includes data gathering.

241. How to Help Teachers Welcome Computers. Geisert, Gene. *American School Board Journal*. v169, n3, p29, Mar 1982.

The author presents an overview of how microcomputers can make the teacher more efficient and effective.

242. If I Had an Apple, What Would I Do with It? Deacon, Jim. *Educational Computer Magazine*. v1, n3, p15, 23, Sep–Oct 1981 (Available from P.O. Box 535, Cupertino, CA 95015).

Reports on a task force of school media personnel in Minnesota that is working on microcomputer applications in school libraries, such as computer assisted library instruction and computer managed circulation.

243. Jim Akin: In French or FORTRAN, His Language Is Success. Sendor, Elizabeth. *Executive Educator*. v3, n10, p15–18, Oct 1981.

Profiles an assistant superintendent of a school district in Alexandria, Virginia and presents his methods of monitoring student progress with achievement test scores and microcomputers.

244. A LEAP (Logistically Efficient Approach) to State Implementation: A Micro Technology-Based Strategy for Technical Assistance. Pogrow, Stanley. *AEDS Journal*. v13, n2, p133–43, Win 1980 (EJ 223 595; Reprint: UMI).

The present approach to providing state assistance to school districts focuses exclusively on conceptual issues and ignores certain critical aspects of physical implementation. The model proposed emphasizes the use of microcomputers in the physical support system and describes an inservice program to train people to use the machines.

245. LOGO: Not Just for Kids. Nelson, Harold. *Kilobaud: Microcomputing*. v6, n3, p96, 98–100, 102, 104–07, Mar 1982.

Although best known for its use with children, LOGO is a programing language with capabilities useful for many applications.

246. Management Applications of the Microcomputer: Promises and Pitfalls. Haugo, John E. *AEDS Journal*. v14, n4, p182–88, Sum 1981.

Examines the advantages and disadvantages of using microcomputers in educational management areas, such as financial, personnel, or student data affairs. Draws a study by MECC to compare microcomputers with large computers and manual record keeping in school administration.

247. Managing Instruction with a Micro. Gundlach, Aly. *Educational Computer Magazine*, v1, n1, p12–15, May-Jun 1981 (Available from P.O. Box 535, Cupertino, CA 95015).

Describes how Washington Elementary School District in Phoenix, Arizona is managing its minimum competency instructional system on Commodore PET microcomputers, using Evans Newton Inc.'s PROJECT BASIC software. Program implementation considerations, such as timelines and inservice teacher education, are discussed.

248. Media Center Spotlight: Please, May I Be Next? Gibbons, Lee. *Educational Computer Magazine*. v2, n2, p21, 50, Mar–Apr 1982.

Presents a brief description of microcomputer usage in a junior high school library.

249. Microcomputer Applications at Ocean View High School Media Center. Sugranes, Maria. *CMLEA Journal*. v43, n2, p9–11, Spr 1980.

The various uses and potential of the Apple II in a high school media center are described.

250. Microcomputer in Colorado—It's Elementary. Costa, Betty. *Wilson Library Bulletin*. v55, n9, p676–717, May 1981 (EJ 247 444; Reprint: UMI).

Describes a microcomputer system at the elementary school level which allows pupils to access information by subject, author, or title, as in a standard card catalog.

251. The Microcomputer Revolution. Fosdick, Howard. *Library Journal*. v105, n13, p1467–72, Jul 1980 (EJ 232 511; Reprint: UMI).

Examines the development of the microcomputer and focuses on its potential for library automation. The characteristics of microcomputers and minicomputers are contrasted, and a selected annotated bibliography includes a list of specialty magazines on microcomputers.

252. Microcomputers and Academic Grading. Strang, Harold R. *Educational Technology*. v20, n10, p58–59, Oct 1980 (EJ 234 635; Reprint: UMI).

Discusses the use of a microprocessor to record, retrieve, edit, and handle grade formulas for students at the University of Virginia.

253. Microcomputers May Be Better for Circ than Minis. The MITRE Corporation. *Library Journal*. v103, n18, p2030–32, Oct 15 1978.

The Metrek Division of The MITRE Corporation has analyzed data from a national survey of packaged (turnkey) circulation systems and has concluded that microcomputers will eventually replace the packaged circulation systems that are now being widely bought by libraries. Copies of *Automated Circulation Systems in Public Libraries* are available from the Metrek Division of The MITRE Corporation, 1820 Dolly Madison Boulevard, McLean, VA 22101.

254. Microcomputers—Tools in Search of Answers.
Johnston, Raymond B. *NASSP Bulletin*. v65, n448,
p122–24, Nov 1981.

The author describes a successful class scheduling program
done with a microcomputer.

255. Microcomputer Use at Wilcox High School. Ward,
Joseph H., Jr. *CMLEA Journal*. v3, n2, p12–14, Spr
1980.

The use of a microcomputer to generate overdue notices for
books in a high school library is described.

256. Microcomputing in an Educational Cooperative.
Brown, R. W. *Kilobaud: Microcomputing*. v5, n10,
p214–17, Oct 1981.

The San Juan, Colorado Board of Cooperative Services is
using Ohio Scientific's C3B with a Winchester disc for test construction, curriculum development, planning, management, and record
keeping.

**257. Program Your Computer to Make Tough Decisions
Easy.** DiGiammarino, Frank P. *Executive Educator*.
v3, n10, p34, Oct 1981 (EJ 252 261; Reprint: UMI).

Describes the data management and analysis system of the
Lexington, Massachusetts public schools. Discusses the system's
database, data dictionary, and end users language. Gives examples
of the system's use in answering questions about school closings.

258. The Role of Microcomputers in Libraries. Lundeen,
Gerald. *Wilson Library Bulletin*. v55, n3, p178–85,
Nov 1980 (EJ 242 777; Reprint: UMI).

Describes the functions and characteristics of the microcomputer. Discusses library applications, including cataloging, circulation, acquisitions, serials control, reference and database systems, administration, current and future trends, and computers as
media. Twenty references are listed.

259. School Business is Going Micro. Costerison, Dennis
L. *School Business Affairs*. v48, n1, p14–15, 28, Jan
1982.

Looks at the advantages of microcomputers for school business applications. Discusses purchasing considerations.

**260. Solving Administrative Problems: Student
Scheduling and Tracking System for the Micro-
computer.** Bolton, Brenda Anthony. *Educational
Computer Magazine*. v2, n2, p24–26, Mar–Apr 1982.

Describes methods of using the microcomputer for student
scheduling and student record keeping.

**261. Someday You'll Use Micros in the Central Office,
Too.** Levin, Dan. *Executive Educator*. v2, n3, p22–
23, Mar 1980.

Outlines the potential of microcomputers in the administration of schools, as well as some of the obstacles to their use.
Concludes that extensive microcomputer use for administrative
purposes is probably several years away.

**262. Special Report: The Computerized Overdue: A
Vade Mecum.** Donovan, Ann. *Wilson Library Bulletin*. v53, n6, p458–59, Feb 1979.

Describes a system whereby a computer program can keep
track of overdue books, saving both time and money.

263. To Register, Talk to This Computer. . . . Spangler,
J. D. *American School and University*. v53, n1, p26–
27, Sep 1980.

Brigham Young University has a talking-listening computer.
Capable of limited conversation, it will be able to register students
by telephone. Programs have also been developed for computer use
in public schools as an aid to teachers.

264. Town and Gown Say I Do. Trippett, B. L. *Instructional Innovator*. v26, n6, p30–31, Sep 1981.

Tells how a group of villages and a small school district in
Rhode Island pooled their resources in order to have access to a
powerful computer.

265. Tracking Student with a Computer. *American
School and University*. v54, n1, p48, Sep 1981 (EJ 251
088; Reprint: UMI).

The Northwestern School of Law at Lewis and Clark College
in Portland, Oregon has a microcomputer installation that now
carries student data from the application process through to a student's admission to the school. Phase two will carry student data
through graduation; phase three will track the graduate's career and
alumni activities.

266. TRYSAL: A Salary Schedule Program. Hamel,
Bob. *The Computing Teacher*. v9, n6, p42–48, Feb
1982.

Provides a listing for a BASIC program that provides data for
negotiating a teacher contract. Salary indexes and fringe benefits are
included. The program was designed for an Apple II computer.

267. The Use of Microcomputers in Libraries. Pratt, Allan D. *Journal of Library Automation*. v13, n1, p7–17,
Mar 1980 (EJ 232 523; Reprint: UMI).

Low-cost and high-capacity microcomputers now have the
potential to improve library services at various levels. They seem
well-adapted for text-processing, preparation of local bibliographies
and resources guides, and for improvement of online database
searching.

**268. Using New Computer Software Products to Manage
and Report Educational Data.** Williams, Warren S.,
et al. *Educational Technology*. v21, n2, p46–51, Feb
1981.

This article has four purposes: (1) to increase readers' awareness of relatively new computer software products that can be used
to maintain, analyze, and report large sets of educational data; (2) to
demonstrate the application of two of those packages to typical
problems faced when manipulating educational data; (3) to provide
administrators with information about evaluating and selecting these
software products; and (4) to encourage project directors to consider
implementing one or more of these new software packages.

MICROFICHE

269. Documentation—INFO: A Small Computer Data Base Management System for School Applications. The Illinois Series on Educational Application of Computers, No. 24e. Cox, John, Illinois University, Urbana, IL. Department of Secondary Education, 1979, 109p. Best copy available. Sponsoring Agency: EXXON Education Foundation, New York, NY.

This paper documents the program used in the application of the INFO system for data storage and retrieval in schools, from the viewpoints of both the unsophisticated user and the experienced programer interested in using the INFO system or modifying it for use within an existing school's computer system. The user's guide presents simple instructions with examples for using the INFO system to store data and search for certain entries. The programer's guide covers size of files and memory needed to use the programs, as well as the time it takes to run the programs. A conversion guideline is included to explain those BASIC language commands which are not always available on other microcomputer systems. A section on each program presents the program listing, the function of each variable, and suggestions for modifications which might be desirable for other applications.

270. The Microcomputer and Management of the Time Bound Educational Program. Mosow, David K.; Hewitt, Thomas W. 1980, 8p. Not available in paper copy due to light print of original document (ED 207 168; Reprint: EDRS).

An example of the application of microcomputers to education, described in this paper, indicates the possibilities for their widespread use. Forecasters claim that microcomputers will be acquired by more and more individuals and families in the 1980s. This implies that schools will also make greater use of microcomputers in computer assisted instruction, school management, and training in computer literacy.

At present, few teacher education programs are training their students in computer usage. A Teacher Corps project at the University of South Alabama uses microcomputers, both to train its students in computers and to help manage the project. As a time-bound program, the project must meet its objectives before its funding ends. Data on staff activities, entered into a microcomputer by staff members, allows the managers to monitor progress toward project objectives, analyze where staff effort is going, and decide which objectives need more staff time. Because of the projects, the university and the local school system have broadened or further investigated their use of microcomputers in both instruction and management.

271. An Overview of MICRO-CMI. McIsaac, Donald, et al. Wisconsin University, Madison, WI, Research and Development Center for Individualized Schooling, Nov 1980, 23p. Sponsoring Agency: National Institute of Education (DHEW), Washington, DC (ED 198 815; Reprint: EDRS).

The MICRO-CMI computer system designed at the University of Wisconsin combines the grouping, diagnosis, and prescription functions of two previously designed systems with the additional dimension of a sheet scanner to input grades and to score tests. Moreover, the user may specify a unique program of studies for each student, thus enabling the support of a special education curriculum designed around Individual Education Programs (IEP). The MICRO-CMI computer in the school offers online generation of results, reports, listings and grading and operates more efficiently than the normal time-sharing system. Since the MICRO-CMI programs have been designed in a modular fashion, new functions can be added with a minimum of effort. Available for distribution on magnetic tape, the computer programs are coded in FORTRAN for a DEC LSI-11, using the RT-11 operating system. Because of the nature of the programing techniques applied and the amount of mass storage required, attempts to implement this program on APPLE. TRS-80, or other small eight-bit computers is not recommended. Sixteen schools in Wisconsin and Illinois participated in a pilot test of the system.

272. The School Administrator's Introduction to Computing. The Illinois Series on Educational Application of Computers, No. 16e. Dennis, J. Richard, Illinois University, Urbana, IL. Department of Secondary Education, 1979, 30p. Best copy available. Sponsoring Agency: EXXON Education Foundation, New York, NY (ED 183 194; Reprint: EDRS).

This discussion of the administrative uses of computers from the perspective of the school administrator is concerned with both the types and sources of information involved in school administration and specific uses of this information. The paper focuses on those administrative tasks that can be effectively computerized in defining the role of the computer for each task. Topics covered include: (1) basic types of information required for school management—student, financial, and personnel; (2) basic models of information flow in schools—"trickle-down" and "percolate-up" models; and (3) selection criteria for computer systems, including software, performance requirements, quality of service estimation, and operating personnel requirements.

Schools seeking to profit from using computers in administration and instruction are advised to concentrate on a similar analysis and definition of information uses and requirements before selecting equipment. This resource for preservice and inservice training includes a listing of a variety of school district database documents and a 27-item bibliography.

273. A Teacher's Introduction to Administrative Uses of Computers. The Illinois Series on Educational Application of Computers, No. 15e. Baum, Madeline, ed., Dennis, J. Richard, ed., Illinois University, Urbana, IL. Department of Secondary Education, 1979, 23p. Best copy available. Sponsoring Agency: EXXON Education Foundation, New York, NY (ED 183 193; Reprint: EDRS).

This paper presents an overview of administrative applications of computers and how they function to help teachers develop the ability to discriminate between well- and poorly-designed methods of using computers to solve administrative problems or accomplish administrative tasks. The administrative applications presented include school financial activities, student information, personnel information, and other management information. Eight problem situations are described as the basis for study activities in administrative uses of computers. Appendix A contains an outline of administrative computer applications in schools; Appendix B contains a list of 25 references. This is one of a series of papers prepared as a resource for preservice and inservice training of teachers.

274. Teaching Elementary Reading by CMI and CAI. Brebner, Ann, et al. 1980, 23p (ED 198 793; Reprint: EDRS).

A computer managed instructional system for reading, begun five years ago in Belvedere-Parkway Elementary School in Calgary, Canada contains 329 behavioral objectives, ranging from kindergarten to eighth-grade levels, with testing performed online. After completion of a test, a student receives a printout listing the objectives completed, those that need revision, and those that remain to be learned. Class reports detail student performance by objectives and provide specific prescriptions for each student related to the reading texts used in the school. Results show that teachers, students, and parents have all benefited. Teachers are freed from administering, scoring, and recording tests and can use the prescriptions to plan individualized instruction. Students are motivated by the positive statements about their progress which appear on their individualized summary sheets together with the objectives which still need work. Parents are pleased because they know, from the summary reports, where their children are in relation to what is expected. In addition, reading achievement scores for sixth-grade students have increased from the 25th to the 55th percentile. Copies of the student summary sheet and the summary report are included.

275. A Title I Refinement: Alaska. Hazelton, Alexander E., et al. Apr 14 1981, 25p. Paper presented at the Annual Meeting of the American Educational Research Association (65th, Los Angeles, CA, Apr 13–17, 1981) (ED 204 381; Reprint: EDRS).

Through joint planning with a number of school districts and the Region X Title I Technical Assistance Center, and with the help of a Title I refinement grant, Alaska has developed a system of data storage and retrieval using microcomputers that assists small school districts in the evaluation and reporting of their Title I programs. Although this system serves as a vehicle for federal and state reporting, its primary function is to help school districts evaluate their own Title I programs. The microcomputer system uses database management techniques, which not only reduce storage requirements, but allow for ad hoc reporting by clerical personnel. This ad hoc reporting capability frees small school districts from being dependent upon having access to programing expertise for producing new or one-time reports. The use of technology in Alaska is described, as is the Title I refinement application program and how it interfaces with the database management system. Examples of ad hoc and standard reports are described.

Selection/Evaluation Criteria

Included in this chapter are citations on needs assessment, aimed at answering such questions as why you should apply selection or evaluation criteria at all until you have assessed whether you need computer capabilities. Most of the literature which discusses needs assessment warns that proposed applications must be the determining factor when deciding on computer hardware or software.

The layperson's definition of software is: If you can type it or load it, it's software. The layperson's definition of hardware is: If you can see it, touch it, smell it, or lift it, it's hardware.

In addition to the needs assessment documents in this section, there are many excellent guides for selecting and evaluating both hardware and software. Many documents scattered throughout this resource guide have a section on hardware and software evaluation and selection, but the documents in this particular section tend to be concrete, straightforward guides to the selection/evaluation process. A number of comparison charts are included.

JOURNAL ARTICLES

276. The ABCs of VDTs. Veit, Stanley. *Personal Computing.* v5, n5, p39, 42–44, 46–49, 120, Aug 1981.

VDT's are reviewed and evaluated. A brief glossary is included.

277. Assessing Inexpensive Microcomputers for Classroom Use: A Product-Oriented Course to Promote Instructional Computing Literacy. Ricketts, Dick; Seay, Jean A. *AEDS Journal.* v13, n1, p89–99, Fall 1979 (EJ 233 575; Reprint: UMI).

A teacher inservice class that focused on evaluating inexpensive microcomputer systems is described. Evaluative criteria used by the class are included, and the findings and preferences of the class are summarized.

278. Choosing a Classroom Microcomputer. Herstein, Ed. *Computing Teacher*. v6, n4, p54–55, May 1979.

A number of microcomputer system characteristics are discussed, and recommendations are made that will help the educator select a system.

279. Choosing a Computer for Education. Smith, Lorraine. *Popular Computing*. v1, n2, p108, Dec 1981.

Computer expert Douglas Gale gives school personnel advice on obtaining small computers, with emphasis on cost-effectiveness and maintenance considerations.

280. Choosing the Right Computer: A General Method. Shetler, Stephen; Shetler, Pauline. *onComputing*. v2, n3, p67–71, Win 1980 (EJ 233 504; Reprint: UMI).

Presents a model procedure for defining one's own computing needs and using that definition to compare the features of various microcomputers.

281. Coming to Terms with Computer Literacy. Klitzner, Carol. *Personal Computing*. v5, n6, p57, 60–61, 64–65, 67, 69–70, 72, Aug 1981.

Examines the trend toward computer literacy instruction in the schools and evaluates four software and one print-based computer literacy packages.

282. The Computer and the English Classroom. Bell, Kathleen. *English Journal*. v69, n9, p88–90, Dec 1980 (EJ 238 448; Reprint: UMI).

Tips on selecting and using microcomputers in the English classroom, along with the reasoning behind the need to become computer literate, are presented.

283. The Computer Shopping Guide. *Instructor*. v89, n8, p88–90, Mar 1980 (EJ 220 473; Reprint: UMI).

This guide provides a chart describing and rating the features of eight 16K microcomputers: Apple II, Atari 800, Commodore PET, Compucolor Mod III, Exidy Sorcerer, Ohio Scientific C4PMF. Tandy TRS-80 Level II, and Texas Instruments 99/4. A glossary of microcomputer terminology and a resource directory are appended.

284. Considerations in Buying a Personal Computer. Zinn, Karl L. *Creative Computing*. v4, n5, p102, Sep–Oct 1978 (EJ 191 260; Reprint: UMI).

This article contains a list of considerations for use by the educator who is interested in buying a personal computer but lacks the technical expertise needed in making such a selection.

285. Disk Memories: What You Should Know before You Buy Them. Bursky, Dave. *Personal Computing*. v5, n4, p20–27, Apr 1981 (Available from Hayden Publishing Company, 50 Essex Street, Rochelle Park, NJ 07662).

Explains the basic features of floppy-disk and hard-disk computer storage systems and the purchasing decisions which must be made, particularly in relation to certain popular microcomputers. A disk vendor directory is included.

286. A Dozen Computers from Which to Choose: What Can You Buy for under $1000? Doll, David M. *Creative Computing*. v7, n9, p18, 20, 22, 26–27, 30, 34–36, Sep 1981 (EJ 251 508; Reprint: UMI).

This article and chart compare 12 computers, priced from $200 to $1,500. The addresses of the 11 manufacturers are provided, along with basic information on each machine.

287. Elementary, My Dear Apple. Schilling, Robert. *Popular Computing*. v1, n1, p78, 80, Nov 1981.

Reviews "Elementary, My Dear Apple," a commercial software package for the Apple II microcomputer. The package contains four computer programs which present elementary-level spelling, math, and economics learning activities in gamelike formats.

288. Evaluating Educational Software. Kleiman, Glenn, et al. *Creative Computing*. v7, n10, p84, 86, 88, 90, Oct 1981 (EJ 252 712; Reprint: UMI).

Explains how to select good educational software. Guidelines are based on general principles that are relevant to a wide variety of teaching programs, topics, students, and computer systems.

289. Evaluation of Instructional Programs for Microcomputers. Judd, Dorothy; Judd, Robert C. *Educational Computer Magazine*. v2, n2, p16–17, Mar–Apr 1982.

The authors emphasize the need to evaluate software. They list resources which provide helpful information for doing so.

290. Friend or Foe? Making the In-House Computer Work for Your School. Ellis, Joseph. *NASSP Bulletin*, v65, n445, p16–23, May 1981.

To promote an understanding of the investigative process, the author divides computer purchasing into six phases: The Romance; The Hardware; The Software; Support Personnel; Staff Training; and The Time Table.

291. General News and Information for the Elementary Grades. Sullivan, Tom. *The Computing Teacher*. v8, n5, p59–61, 1980–81.

Addresses the argument that K-8 software is insufficient in quantity and quality by describing courseware development efforts of independent groups and three major publishers: Random House, Inc., Scott, Foresman and Co., and Science Research Associates.

292. Getting Hard-Nosed about Software: Guidelines for Evaluating Computerized Instructional Materials. Kansky, Bob, et al. *Mathematics Teacher*. v74, n8, p600–04, Nov 1981.

This article is an overview of the major issues raised in "Guidelines for Evaluating Computerized Instructional Materials," a document prepared by the National Council of Teachers of Mathematics.

293. The Golden Rule and Ten Commandments of Computer Based Education (CBE). Aiken, Robert M. *Technological Horizons in Education*, v8, n3, p39–42, Mar 1981 (EJ 252 824; Reprint: UMI).

Examines 10 factors that people selecting and using computers in the classroom should consider if the system is to be effectively used as a teaching tool. Topics include personnel, materials, services, and equipment.

294. Help!!! What Computer Should I Buy? Braun, Ludwig. *Mathematics Teacher*. v7, n8, p593–98, Nov 1981.

Suggests a set of criteria that is useful in deciding which computer to buy and provides a rational way of applying these criteria to all computers under consideration.

295. How Do I Choose a Personal Computer? Braun, Ludwig. *AEDS Journal*. v13, n1, p81–87, Fall 1979 (EJ 223 574; Reprint: UMI).

The decision-making approach outlined involves defining a vector of computer characteristics, which are modified by importance factors and by assessments of the extent to which each computer realizes each of the characteristics. A single number that may be regarded as a "figure of merit" results.

296. How $600 Can Get You Going on a VDT System. Warren, John. *Journalism Educator*. v35, n1, p11–12, Apr 1980 (EJ 225 233; Reprint: UMI).

Recommends the use of an inexpensive TRS-80 system that can be adapted to simulate many of the electronic editing functions of a VDT. Points out some of its limitations but emphasizes the significant savings involved.

297. How to Buy Microcomputers . . . and How & Where to Use Them. Carter, Jim A., Jr. *School Shop*. v40, n8, p28–33, Apr 1981 (EJ 241 922; Reprint: UMI).

Discusses factors to consider when selecting microcomputers for school use, including components, cost, reliability, serviceability, type of user, applications, input and output requirements, processing, and storage. Also describes the development of a computer area for a multiple activity lab.

298. How to Make the Right Decisions about Microcomputers. Milner, Stuart D. *Instructional Innovator*. v25, n6, p12–19, Sep 1980 (EJ 232 615; Reprint: UMI).

Details factors related to the selection of microcomputer systems for computer based instruction, including cost-effectiveness, instruction improvement and enhancement, and projected use. Descriptions of Apple, Atari, PET, Sorcerer, TERAK, Texas Instruments, and TRS-80 are included, along with a glossary of microcomputer related terms.

299. How to Start a Software Exchange. Lathrop, Ann; Goodson, Bobby. *Recreational Computing*. v10, n2, p24–26, Sep–Oct 1981 (Available from People's Computer Company, Box E, Menlo Park, CA 94025).

Describes the microcomputer display center and SOFTSWAP program developed by the San Mateo County, California Office of Education and the Computer Using Educators' group. SOFTSWAP disseminates teacher-produced, public domain courseware and is beginning evaluations of commercial products.

300. How We Do It: Microcomputers—How Do You Get Started? Larson, Lee E. *Journal of College Science Teaching*. v10, n4, p231–33, Feb 1981 (EJ 241 097; Reprint: UMI).

Discusses single-board microcomputers, designed primarily for data acquisition and control. Directed toward individuals with little or no hands-on experience with microcomputers, this article gives references on a variety of aspects, including reading about and purchasing microcomputers.

301. Micros—User Considerations. Bauman, Ben M.; Brooks, Lloyd D. *Educational Computer Magazine*. v1, n3, p32–33, 37, Sep–Oct 1981.

The reader is warned to let proposed applications be the determining factor when selecting a computer system.

302. Modems: Your Line to the World. Veit, Stanley; Gabel, David. *Personal Computing*. v5, n9, p90–92, 94, 96–97, 99–100, 102, Sep 1981.

Modems are thoroughly explained. A chart comparing popular personal computer modems is included.

303. A New Exec Toy? Stein, Donna. *Working Woman*. v7, n1, p59–63, Jan 1982.

When introduced, microcomputers were aimed at specialists and sophisticated hobbyists. Personal computers are now marketed as the managerial tool of the 80s. Tips for novice users, costs, and brief descriptions of seven popular microcomputer models are presented.

304. News. *Technological Horizons in Education*. v7, n6, p14–16, Nov 1980.

Reports on the rationale for standardizing the purchase of microcomputers by the Houston Independent School District; the general criteria used to evaluate bids; and the reasons why Bell & Howell was selected as the best bidder. This is the largest single microcomputer purchase by a school district to date.

305. Personal Computer Comparison Chart. North, Steve. *Creative Computing*. v5, n11, p30–31, Nov 1979 (EJ 213 193; Reprint: UMI).

Six personal computers are rated on 18 features, ranging from memory and language to price.

306. Personal Computers: Products for Every Need. *Personal Computing*. v5, n5, p45–55, 74, May 1981 (Available from Hayden Publishing Company, 50 Essex Street, Rochelle Park, NJ 07662).

Begins a two-part look at some of the personal computers now on the market. Discusses microcomputers being offered by Apple, Atari, Commodore (PET), Heath, Hewlett-Packard, Ohio Scientific, Osborne, Radio Shack (TRS-80), and Texas Instruments.

307. The Potential Is Great: Problems and Possibilities for Computer-Assisted Instruction. Callison, William. *NASSP Bulletin*. v65, n445, p24–28, May 1981 (EJ 243 858; Reprint: UMI).

Four systems for computer assisted instruction—PLATO, TICCIT, TRS-80, and Apple II—are explained and compared.

308. Primer for Purchasing Computer Programs: Part 2. Delf, Robert M. *American School and University.* v51, n1, p30–31, Sep 1981 (EJ 251 081; Reprint: UMI).

The second article in a series of three aimed at helping purchasers obtain the best computer programs for their budgets, deals with bid solicitation and software evaluation. The first article appeared in the July 1981 issue.

309. Problems in Selecting a Microcomputer for Educational Applications. Matthews, John I. *AEDS Journal.* v13, n1, p69–79, Fall 1979 (EJ 223 573; Reprint: UMI).

Examines the problems in selecting a microcomputer and offers suggestions on choosing equipment and on procedures to follow in making a decision.

310. Selecting Microcomputers for the Classroom. Thomas, David B.; McClain, Donald H. *AEDS Journal.* v13, n1, p55–68, Fall 1979 (EJ 223 572; Reprint: UMI).

Outlines a model that will help teachers perform the prerequisite activities necessary for the specification of a microcomputer system that will meet present and future instructional computing needs.

311. Shopping for Technology: Three Educators Tell What They'd Buy—and Why. Keener, Thomas. *Electronic Learning.* v1, n1, p29–31, 58–62, Sep–Oct 1981.

Given a hypothetical $10,000, three educators tell what microcomputer hardware and software they would buy. Budget charts are included.

312. Should Your Next Terminal Be a Computer? Pemberton, Jeffery K. *Database.* v4, n3, p4–6, Sep 1981.

Presents reasons why microcomputers are a better investment than simply upgrading to a plain video terminal. Gives advice on how to shop for that first microcomputer.

313. So You Want to Buy a Computer? Wood, R. Kent; Wooley, Robert D. *Instruction.* v89, n8, p86, Mar 1980 (EJ 220 472; Reprint: UMI).

Presents a list of questions about costs and program needs that an educator should consider before purchasing a microcomputer.

314. Stalking Microcomputer Software. Glotfelty, Ruth. *School Library Journal.* v28, n7, p91–94, Mar 1982.

Describes the Pontiac Township High School media center's attempt to preview software, despite the reluctance of microcomputer software producers to allow previewing. The attempt was largely successful.

315. A Successful Transition from Mini- to Microcomputer-Assisted Instruction: The Norfolk Experience. Gull, Randall L. *Educational Technology.* v20, n12, p41–42, Dec 1980 (EJ 240 860; Reprint: UMI).

Reviews reasons for the decision to change from a time-share minicomputer to microcomputers. Looks at the financial considerations involved; the purchase of hardware; the problem posed by the lack of compatible software for the microcomputers; and the development of AIDS for adapting minicomputer software and authoring additional lessons.

316. The Texas Instruments 99/4 Personal Computer. Morgan, Chris. *onComputing.* v2, n2, p29–30, 32–33, Fall 1980 (EJ 229 350; Reprint: UMI).

This product review describes and evaluates the features of the TI 99/4, including its speech synthesizer, its costs, peripherals, and software.

317. These Experts Can Wake You from the Software Nightmare. Levin, Dan. *Executive Educator.* v4, n3, p26, 28, Mar 1982.

Hardheaded advice is given by school executives and computer users who have faced the problem of poor-quality software.

318. Three New TRS-80 Computers: A Product Report. Miastkowski, Stan. *onComputing.* v2, n3, p8–10, 12–15, Win 1980 (EJ 233 502; Reprint: UMI).

Presents product characteristics, costs, and a personal evaluation of Radio Shack's three new personal computers: the TRS-80 Model III; the TRS-80 Color Computer; and the TRS-80 Pocket Computer.

319. Today's Personal Computers: Products for Every Need—Part II. *Personal Computing.* v5, n6, p9–10, 13–15, 73–75, Jun 1981 (Available from Hayden Publishing Company, 50 Essex Street, Rochelle Park, NJ 07662).

Looks at microcomputers manufactured by Altos Computer Systems, Cromemco, Exidy, Intelligent Systems, Intertec Data Systems, Mattel, Nippon Electronics, Northstar, Personal Micro Computers, and Sinclair. Part one of this article, examining other computers, appeared in the May 1981 issue.

320. 12 Questions to Answer before Buying a Computer. Garritano, Raymond J. *American School Board Journal.* v168, n9, p34, 42, Sep 1981 (EJ 251 020; Reprint: UMI).

Offers guidelines and a checklist to use when buying a computer.

321. Van Helps Schools Select the Right Computer. Staples, Betsy. *Creative Computing.* v7, n3, p106–12, Mar 1981 (EJ 244 591; Reprint: UMI).

Guidelines designed to aid in a systematic approach to the selection of hardware and software for classroom use are presented. This material is a part of the information provided by a Multi Media Training Van, supported by the Pennsylvania Department of Education.

322. What About Those Electronic Games? Bitter, Gary. *Teacher.* v97, n3, p78–82, Nov–Dec 1979 (EJ 222 830; Reprint: UMI).

The author looks at the educational merits of some of the new hand-held computer games, such as "The Little Professor," "Speak and Spell," and "Astrowar." Games are grouped in five categories: mathematics; spelling and words; pattern-logic; strategy sports games; and miscellaneous. Manufacturers and prices are provided.

323. **What a Smart Terminal Can Do for You.** Cobb, Allen. *onComputing*. v3, n1, p62–64, 66, 68, 70, Sum 1981.

Presents capabilities to look for when exploring the world of serial terminals to improve or expand a system.

324. **Which Computer Is for You?** Staples, Betsy. *Creative Computing*. v7, n9, p12, 14, Sep 1981 (EJ 251 507; Reprint: UMI).

Presents some guidelines for making intelligent selections when buying computers. The intended primary use of the equipment is seen as the major point to consider when planning the purchase. Other important points to consider and possible sources of relevant information are noted.

325. **Your Own Computer: Buyers Guide to Home Computers.** *Radio-Electronics*. v51, n10, p47–84, Oct 1980.

Takes a thorough look at six popular microcomputers, as well as peripherals and accessories.

MICROFICHE

326. **Checklist/Guide to Selecting a Small Computer.** Bennett, Wilma E., Pilot Industries, New York, NY, 1980, 33p (ED 192 814; Reprint: EDRS; also available from Pilot Books, 347 5th Avenue, New York, NY 10016).

This 322-point checklist was designed to help executives make an intelligent choice when selecting a small computer for a business. For ease of use, the questions have been divided into 10 categories: display features, keyboard features, printer features, controller features, software, word processing, service, training, miscellaneous, and costs. To use the checklist, one reads through the entire list of questions, lining out those which do not apply to a particular business. The remaining items are then categorized to see if they are considered "essential" (E) or "nice-to-have" (N). Equipment from three different vendors can be compared by making check marks in the spaces provided to the right of each question. By completing this checklist, the user can determine which computer company comes closest to satisfying his/her needs. A glossary of computer terms, containing 163 items of jargon frequently found in computer advertisements, is included.

327. **Computer Assisted Instruction in Schools: Achievements, Present Developments, and Projections for the Future.** Hallworth, H.J.; Brebner, Ann, Calgary University, Calgary, AB, Canada. Faculty of Education, Jun 1980, 243p. Sponsoring Agency: Alberta Department of Education, Edmonton, AB, Canada. Planning and Research Branch (ED 200 187; Reprint: EDRS).

This overview of CAI traces the development and use of computers in learning and instruction and describes some current CAI projects, including PLATO, CDC PLATO, and TICCIT. Also discusses CAI projects at Stanford University, the Computer Curriculum Corporation, and in Chicago, Los Nietos, California, Minnesota, Europe, and Canada. Examines technological developments in microcomputers and their use for CAI; hard copy, display terminals, and multimedia terminals for CAI; videotape; videodisc; and communications. Also examines factors influencing the future development of CAI, such as costs; student achievement and attitude; integration of CAI into the instructional setting; and CAI languages. Conclusions and recommendations are concerned with hardware, software, courseware, personnel, CAI priority areas, and demonstration projects. An extensive bibliography is provided, and additional remarks on CAI languages and a schedule of visits made in connection with the study are appended.

328. **Computer Assisted Instruction in Schools: Achievements, Present Developments, and Projections for the Future, Executive Summary.** Hallworth, H. J.; Brebner, Ann, Calgary University, Calgary, AB, Canada. Faculty of Education (ED 200 188; Reprint: EDRS).

This summary report focuses on the hardware which has been used in the major projects detailed in the complete report and new delivery systems for CAI that are currently available or being developed. The need for additional software for microcomputers is pointed out, some advantages and applications of CAI are briefly reviewed, and the establishment of CAI demonstration projects in schools and school districts is recommended, with priority given to students and subject areas most likely to benefit from CAI.

329. **Evaluating Materials for Teaching with a Computer, The Illinois Series on Educational Application of Computers, No. 5e.** Dennis, J. Richard, Illinois University, Urbana, IL. Department of Secondary Education, 1979, 26p. Best copy available. Sponsoring Agency: EXXON Education Foundation, New York, NY (ED 183 185; Reprinted: EDRS).

The details and process of evaluating computerized instructional materials are presented for the major types of such materials, i.e., courseware (the set of computer programs with which the student interacts directly to learn) and instructional software (the instructional facilities, services, or general operations which include management and testing). Formative and summative appraisals, both used to evaluate conventional materials, are considered appropriate. However, two different points of focus are indicated for use with computerized materials: the interaction focus and the subject matter focus. The interaction focus concentrates both on the mechanical aspects of interaction, such as the function of keyboards, and such logical and communication aspects of interaction as the dialog with the student and the degree of individualization. The subject matter focus concentrates on analysis of the content, terminology, topic organization, teaching strategies, choice of examples, etc. The questions to be asked and the data to be gathered are provided for evaluating materials in each class, but it is pointed out that firsthand experiences are mandatory to get a true measure of the characteristics and usefulness of any instructional computing program. This resource for preservice and inservice teacher training includes a study activity, two references, and a courseware evaluation worksheet.

330. Evaluator's Guide for Microcomputer-Based Instructional Packages. Northwest Regional Educational Laboratory, Portland, OR, 1981, 61p. Developed by MicroSIFT, A Project of Computer Technology Program. Sponsoring Agency: National Institute of Education (ED), Washington, DC (ED 206 330; Reprint: EDRS).

This guide, developed by MicroSIFT, a clearinghouse for microcomputer based educational software and courseware, provides background information and forms to aid teachers and other educators in evaluating available microcomputer courseware. The evaluation process consists of four states: (1) sifting, which screens out those programs that are not instructional in nature and determines a package's operational readiness and hardware compatibility; (2) package description, including program format, instructional purpose and technique, type of package, available documentation, and the hardware configuration necessary for operation; (3) courseware evaluation, i.e., an assessment of the content, instructional quality, and technical quality of the package; and (4) in-depth evaluation, which is not described in this guide. Forms for the second and third phases are provided, together with explanations of the kinds of information needed and discussions of some of the factors to be considered in completing certain sections of the forms. Definitions of 15 terms are provided in the introductory section.

331. Getting Started in School Computing: Preparing to Purchase. The Illinois Series on Educational Application of Computers, No. 14e. Dennis, J. Richard; Muiznieks, Viktors, Illinois University, Urbana, IL. Department of Secondary Education, 1979, 31p. Best copy available. Sponsoring Agency: EXXON Education Foundation, New York, NY (ED 183 192; Reprint: EDRS).

This paper identifies concerns and provides guidelines for the administrator or teacher who is involved in making decisions about acquiring, maintaining, or expanding computer resources. Several questions are raised; topics that focus attention on specific elements in a system which are pertinent to procurement are discussed. Major questions are raised concerning the meeting of user needs, resource appropriateness, efficiency, equipment acquisition, and software procurement. A 28-item bibliography is attached.

332. Guide to Microcomputers. Frederick, Franz J., Association for Educational Communications and Technology, Washington, DC; ERIC Clearinghouse on Information Resources, Syracuse, NY, 1980, 159p. Sponsoring Agency: National Institute of Education (DHEW), Washington, DC (ED 192 818; Reprint: EDRS; also available from AECT Publications Sales, 1126 16th Street, N.W., Washington, DC 20036.

This comprehensive guide to microcomputers and their role in education discusses the general nature of microcomputers; computer languages in simple English; operating systems and what they can do; compatible systems; special accessories; service and maintenance; computer assisted instruction, computer managed instruction, and computer graphics; time-sharing and resource-sharing; potential instructional and media center applications; and special applications, e.g., electronic mail, networks, and videodiscs. Available resources are presented in a bibliography of magazines and journals about microcomputers and software and their uses. Addi-

tional resources can be found in a selected list of companies specializing in creating specialized languages and applications programs for microcomputers, and a selected list of companies specializing in the preparation of educational programs for use on microcomputers.

333. Instructional Software Selection: A Guide to Instructional Microcomputer Software. Microcomputers in Education Series. Douglas, Shirley; Neights, Gary, Pennsylvania State Department of Education, Harrisburg, PA, 33p (ED 205 201; Reprint: EDRS).

This guide for evaluating microcomputer instructional software includes a hardware/software interface analysis sheet, which can be used to determine if the software being evaluated is compatible with the hardware on which it will be used. Also provided is an instructional software evaluation form for use in making judgments about: (1) specific instructional objectives; (2) grade level; (3) validation data; (4) correlation data; (5) instructional design features. Appendices include a listing of seven computer users' groups and local computer clubs in California, Ohio, and Pennsylvania; a bibliography of resources; and a list of organizations concerned with computer assisted instruction. A glossary of terms dealing specifically with microcomputer software is also appended.

334. Microcomputer Guide. Pors, George, ed., North Dakota State Department of Public Instruction, Bismarck, ND, Sep 1979, 51p (ED 205 169; Reprint: EDRS).

Designed for use by school districts introducing computer mathematics into the curriculum, this manual provides guidelines for selecting a microcomputer system, as well as objectives and an outline for an introductory course in computer programing. Also presented are topics for computer applications in science, mathematics, chemistry, and physics, and three computer programs: (1) STAR PROBE, used to demonstrate the effects of gravitation and changes in velocity components; (2) Coefficients of Friction; and (3) Elemental Ratios for Empirical Formulas. Resources listed include textbooks on computer programing, references, periodicals, and a glossary of computer terminology. Programing information for a CAI spelling program, a descriptive outline of computer related careers, and an introduction to flow charting (with examples) are appended.

335. Microcomputer Reference: A Guide to Microcomputers. Microcomputers in Education Series. Douglas, Shirley; Neights, Gary, Pennsylvania State Department of Education, Harrisburg, PA, 1980, 37p (ED 205 203; Reprint: EDRS).

This guide for educational practitioners who are considering the purchase of a microcomputer provides a brief discussion of basic information about computers, some criteria to use in conducting a needs assessment prior to the purchase of any microcomputer equipment, and criteria for use in the evaluation of various microcomputers in relation to the needs of the purchaser. Both a needs assessment instrument and evaluation worksheets are included, as well as a glossary of computer terms; a list of microcomputer related organizations, associations, consortia, and networks; a list of relevant periodicals; and a 13-item bibliography.

336. Some Bases for Choosing a Computer System: Suggestions for Educators. Technical Report No. 2. Braun, Ludwig, State University of New York, Stony Brook, NY. College of Engineering, Aug 1, 1978, 52p. Photographs and drawings of computers will not reproduce well. Sponsoring Agency: National Institute of Education (DHEW), Washington, DC (ED 191 732; Reprint: EDRS).

This report reviews four different computer systems that are available for educational use. Presented is a system overview, and the strengths and weaknesses of each of the following systems: PLATO, TERAK, Compucolor II, and PET. Each of these machines is included as a representative of a "class" of machines available to the educator. Their selection for review is not intended as an endorsement but, rather, to permit specificity in discussions of properties. The report looks at the characteristics of each of these machines, as they pertain to educational applications, to aid educators in evaluating computer systems and in making a good choice from among the multitude of systems offered in the marketplace. This document concludes with a comparison among these four computers, based upon a set of 25 educationally important parameters and a glossary of technical computer related terms.

BOOKS

337. Guidelines for Evaluating Computerized Instructional Materials. Heck, William P., et al. National Council of Teachers of Mathematics, Inc., Reston, VA, 1981, 30p (Available from National Council of Teachers of Mathematics, 1906 Association Drive, Reston, VA 22091).

This guide, prepared under the direction of the Instructional Affairs Committee of the National Council of Teachers of Mathematics (NCTM), is designed to serve all educators interested in the instructional applications of computers. Its development has been marked by a continuous, conscious effort to address the needs of all educators, regardless of their areas of interest, subject matter, or present level of involvement with instructional computing. The guide meets three needs: (1) it provides information about the location, selection, and evaluation of computerized materials; (2) it reports this information in small sections; and (3) it defines five paths for using the guide, called "tour groups," in terms of the reader's instructional computing skills and goals. The sections to the

guide are titled: (1) "A Guide to These Guidelines"; (2) "What, Why, and for Whom"; (3) "Obtaining Software and Documentation"; (4) "Getting Hardnosed about Software: Guidelines for Software Review"; (5) "Communicating with Posterity: Guidelines for Software Documentation", (6) "Asides to the Instructional Programer"; (7) "Next Steps"; and (8) "Extra Forms."

338. Microcomputer Courseware/Microprocessor Games. EPIE Report Number 98/99m. Educational Products Information Exchange Institute, New York, NY: EPIE Institute, 1981, 54p (Available from EPIE Institute, 475 Riverside Drive, New York, NY 10027).

The EPIE report addresses the issue of what makes effective instructional software for the microcomputer. Included are a description of the ongoing evaluation project that EPIE is conducting, six comprehensive analyses and evaluations of large commercial courseware packages, and conclusions about the current state of the art.

The report focuses on the criteria that are considered essential in the design of courseware for the microcomputer. Also of concern are the qualities unique to the microcomputer which should be exploited to maximize its instructional potential. For instance, one of the most exciting features of the microcomputer for instruction is its capability to interact with the learner, to respond to the learner's individual, immediate needs. Educators must also bear in mind that the microcomputer will not solve every instructional problem, nor is it most appropriately used as an elaborate workbook.

By realizing the exact capabilities and limitations of the microcomputer, educators will become better consumers and users of the software. Once aware of what constitutes good instructional design and an effective program, consumers have an opportunity to directly shape the microcomputer courseware market by demanding high-quality programs.

339. Practical Guide to Computers in Education. Coburn, Peter, et al. Reading, MA: Addison-Wesley Publishing Company, 1982, 266p.

Spanning all grade levels and subject areas, this book is filled with practical tips, techniques, and recommendations for the introduction and use of microcomputers in the classroom. It covers choosing a computer system, choosing the software, and integrating computers into the schools. Discusses both the serious problems and great promises facing education in general and educational computing in particular. Included are an appendix (with comparison charts), a bibliography, additional resources, and a glossary.

Teacher/Administrator Education

The documents in this section, whether discussing preservice or inservice education, also include administrator education. The rationale behind this is that the administrator, when being trained to be computer literate, is acting in the generic role of "educator," rather than in the specific role of "administrator." Also, regardless of whether a document deals with teaching teachers about literacy or with developing curriculum (software), it has been placed in the "Teacher/Administrator Education" section.

As the reader will see if s/he browses through this section, the number of citations listed is small, because relatively little has been published on the topic of teacher education.

JOURNAL ARTICLES

340. **Certification of Pre-College Teachers of Computing.** Hector, Judith H. *The Computing Teacher*. v8, n4, p43–45, 1980–81.

Presents a list of those states with some certification of computer oriented teachers.

341. **Computers Are for Kids: Designing Software Programs to Avoid Problems of Learning.** Grimes, Lynn. *Teaching Exceptional Children*. v14, n2, p49–53, Nov 1981.

Procedures for programing computers to deal with handicapped students; problems in selective attention; visual discrimination; reaction time differences; short-term memory; transfer and generalization; recognition of mistakes; and social skills are discussed.

342. **Computer Technology and Teacher Education.** Podemski, Richard S. *Journal of Teacher Education*. v32, n1, p29–33, Jan–Feb 1981.

Presents four strategies for colleges of education to use in responding to the need for computer sophistication within teacher education programs. The author warns of the danger of not recognizing the impact of computers on education.

343. **Developing Computer Educational Skills: An Inservice Training Program.** Diem, Richard A. *Educational Technology*. v21, n2, p30–32, Feb 1981.

Presents a brief description of a staff development program in computer literacy.

344. **How Educators Can Become Computer Literates.** Myers, Arlene. *The Computing Teacher*. v8, n3, p34–42, 1980–81.

Lists five concerns educators have about computer literacy: obtaining the money, training teachers, finding high-quality courseware, ensuring that computing knowledge is properly used, and becoming too dependent on computing. Also includes suggestions to help teachers find assistance; organizations committed to helping teachers use computers in the classroom; an annotated book list; and a list of some textbooks addressing the problems of introducing computers into the curriculum.

345. **How Educators Perceive Computers in the Classroom.** Stevens, Dorothy Jo. *AEDS Journal*. v13, n3, p221–32, Spr 1980 (EJ 227 889; Reprint: UMI).

Among the findings of this survey, conducted to assess the knowledge and attitudes of Nebraska K-12 teachers, Teachers College faculty, and student teachers, was that the educators strongly favor instruction to foster computer literacy in secondary schools. However, respondents did not feel qualified to teach the classes.

346. **How to Introduce Teachers, Principals and Curriculum Personnel to the Microcomputer.** Hedges, William D. *The Computing Teacher*. v8, n5, p45–46, 1980–81.

Presents tips for working with the adult learner in a programing class.

347. **Introduction to Computers in Education for Elementary and Middle School Teachers—Chapter 1.** Moursund, David. *The Computing Teacher*, v8, n3, p6–11, 1980.

This first installment begins the serialization of a book designed to provide teachers with what they really need to know about computers. (See also following articles.)

348. Introduction to Computers in Education for Elementary and Middle School Teachers—Chapter 2. Moursund, David. *The Computing Teacher.* v8, n3, p7–19, 1980–81.

This chapter focuses on a technical overview and purposes of the computer.

349. Introduction to Computers in Education for Elementary and Middle School Teachers—Chapter 3. Moursund, David. *The Computing Teacher.* v8, n5, p26–34, 1980–81.

This chapter focuses on student activities. Exercises are included.

350. Introduction to Computers in Education for Elementary and Middle School Teachers—Chapter 4. Moursund, David. *The Computing Teacher.* v8, n6, p13–21, 1980–81.

The focus of this chapter is on games and exercises, including ''hidden treasure'' and ''tic-tac-toe.''

351. Introduction to Computers in Education for Elementary and Middle School Teachers—Chapter 5. Moursund, David. *The Computing Teacher.* v8, n7, p11–18, 1980–81.

This chapter begins by discussing the history of symbols and then focuses on numeration systems.

352. Introduction to Computers in Education for Elementary and Middle School Teachers—Chapter 6. Moursund, David. *The Computing Teacher.* v9, n1, p15–24, Sep 1981.

This chapter focuses on problem solving in a computer environment, describing the steps in programing to solve a problem. Exercises and activities are included.

353. Introduction to Computers in Education for Elementary and Middle School Teachers—Chapter 7. Moursund, David. *The Computing Teacher.* v9, n2, p15–24, Oct 1981.

This chapter focuses on computer and information science, modeling and simulation, information retrieval, computer graphics, and artificial intelligence.

354. Making the Transition to Computers Easy: Steps to Take in Inservice Training. Johnson, J. Rykken. *Educational Computer Magazine.* v1, n2, p16–19, Jul–Aug 1981.

The author makes many useful suggestions to teachers who are wondering how to ''get ready, get set, and go.''

355. Microcomputers in the Service of Students and Teachers—Computer-Assisted Instruction at the California School for the Deaf: An Update. Arcanin, Jacob; Zawolkow, Geoffrey. *American Annals of the Deaf.* v125, n6, p807–13, Sep 1980 (EJ 236 809; Reprint: UMI).

A regional center had been established that focuses on training teachers to develop computerized lessons. The lessons are categorized and stored in a lesson library to which all teachers have access.

356. Organizing Computer Assisted Instructional Programs. Savage, Earl R. *80 Microcomputing.* n17, p54, 57, May 1981.

Presents simple steps a teacher should take when planning to write a CAI program.

357. Overcoming Educators' Fear about Classroom Computers. Morrissey, Willis J., Jr. *The Computing Teacher.* v8, n2, p50–51, 1980–81.

Provides tips for overcoming resistance during an introductory course for teachers on CAI.

358. A Paradigm of Computer Literacy Training for Teachers. Beck, John J., Jr. *The Computing Teacher.* v9, n2, p27–28, Oct 1981.

Suggests content for a one-day workshop and a full-scale course to introduce teachers to computers.

359. Pennsylvania's Statewide Initiative. Neights, Gary. *Instructional Innovator.* v26, n6, p26–27, Sep 1981.

Propelled by Secretary of Education Robert G. Scanlon, Pennsylvania's administrators, media specialists, and media technicians are becoming computer literate.

360. School Administrator's Introduction to Instructional Use of Computers. Moursund, David. *The Computing Teacher.* v8, n2, p8–22, 1980–81.

This article presents an introduction to computers in education for school administrators and school board members who have little knowledge of instructional uses of computers.

361. Teaching Computer Literacy: Guidelines for a Six-Week Course for Teachers. Anderson, Cheryl. *Electronic Learning.* v1, n2, p30–31, Nov–Dec 1981.

Presents helpful suggestions for setting up an inservice course to teach teachers about computers.

362. Teaching Teachers about Computers: A Necessity for Education. Milner, Stuart D. *Phi Delta Kappan.* v61, n8, p544–46, Apr 1980 (EJ 219 582; Reprint: UMI).

Offers a framework for contemplating teacher education in computer use. Includes brief descriptions of suggested courses for a teacher education program and types of teacher education activities.

363. Using Computer-Wise Students . . . Wisely. Gass, Stephen. *Electronic Learning.* v1, n1, p26–27, Sep–Oct 1981.

Presents a look at a school that is providing its computer using faculty with a 12-person resource staff for free—by using students as computer aides.

MICROFICHE

364. Computer Managed Instruction and Individualization. The Illinois Series on Educational Application of Computers, No. 11e. Dennis, J. Richard, Illinois University, Urbana, IL. Department of Secondary Education, 1979, 31p. Best copy available. Sponsoring Agency: EXXON Education Foundation, New York, NY (ED 183 190; Reprint: EDRS).

This paper describes functions of a computer system for management of individualized instruction; provides details of a CMI facility, explains the role of the teacher in utilizing a CMI system; and lists five programs which implement the concept of individualization with computer assistance. CMI system functions described include diagnosing, assigning or prescribing, facilitating study, evaluating, collecting and manipulating data, reporting, managing resources and space, providing an information network, and implementing materials. The computerized facilities which comprise a system are also described, including materials creation, individualized study/evaluation, records and reporting, resource management, and communication. A brief discussion of the teacher's role in CMI and a review of CMI systems—PLAN, TIPS, CISS, AIS, and TICCIT—are included. This resource for preservice and inservice teacher training includes study activities and a 31-item bibliography.

365. Computers in the Curriculum. Fastback 82. Baker, Justine, Phi Delta Kappa Educational Foundation, Bloomington, IN, 1976, 45p. Contains occasional small print (ED 133 166; Reprint: EDRS; also available from Phi Delta Kappa, Eighth and Union, Box 789, Bloomington, IN 47401).

This publication discusses computer education for teachers, reports the results of a nationwide survey on what teacher training institutions are doing about computer education, and looks into computer education trends in American school districts. Results of a national survey of superintendents' attitudes concerning the role of the computer in the classroom and the training of teachers using computers for instruction are briefly discussed. An annotated bibliography on the use of computers in education is included.

366. Designing Instruction for Teaching with a Computer. The Illinois Series on Educational Application of Computers, No. 3e. Alessi, Stephen M.; Dennis, J. Richard, Illinois University, Urbana, IL. Department of Secondary Education, 1979, 28p. Sponsoring Agency: EXXON Education Foundation, New York, NY (ED 183 183; Reprint: EDRS).

A review of the major components of lesson planning and two conventional planning methods provides background for this explanation of the type of planning required when designing instruction for teaching with the computer. This ''formal planning'' includes identification and articulation of the logical sequencing of both instructional events and instructional decisions; planning sequences are nonlinear, taking a flowchart form, rather than being tightly tied to the days of the week. Discussion of the factors involved in formal planning includes consideration of decisions as instructional events, sequencing based on decisions, the organization of formal planning, and construction of the flowchart. Examples of first and second

drafts of a flowchart for a series of lessons teaching the computer language BASIC are provided. This document was designed as a resource for preservice and inservice teacher training. A study activity is provided, as well as a list of seven references.

367. Drill and Practice on a Computer. The Illinois Series on Educational Application of Computers, No. 7e. Steward, James I., Illinois University, Urbana, IL. Department of Secondary Education, 1979, 24p. Best copy available. Sponsoring Agency: EXXON Education Foundation, New York, NY (ED 183 187; Reprint: EDRS).

When designing a computerized drill and practice lesson, the teacher should (1) select the content and processes of the lesson to match the content and processes of the initial instruction; (2) present a variety of stimulus presentations for an item; (3) select constructed or nonconstructed response modes, depending on the type and complexity of the material being practiced; (4) provide appropriate feedback for a student's response; (5) systematically select the next appropriate item to be presented; (6) have some appropriate lesson termination strategy; and (7) update records and report the student's score in some meaningful manner. A sample program of a general drill-and-practice lesson is presented and described. This resource for preservice and inservice teacher training provides study questions and a 14-item bibliography.

368. The Question Episode—Building Block of Teaching with a Computer. The Illinois Series on Educational Application of Computers, No. 4e. Dennis, J. Richard, Illinois University, Urbana, IL. Department of Secondary Education, 1979, 16p. Sponsoring Agency: EXXON Education Foundation, New York, NY (ED 183 184; Reprint: EDRS).

This paper presents the notion of a ''question episode,'' the smallest complete unit of computer/student interaction in computer assisted instruction and describes such important elements as question types, student input, interpretation of student inputs, computer replies, and duration limits. Includes guidelines to help determine the quality of question episodes found in computerized lessons. This resource for preservice and inservice teacher training suggests two study activities and lists one reference.

369. Teacher Education in Use of Computers. The Illinois Series on Educational Application of Computers, No. 1e. Dennis, J. Richard, Illinois University, Urbana, IL. Department of Secondary Education, 1979, 23p. Sponsoring Agency: EXXON Education Foundation, New York (ED 183 181; Reprint: EDRS).

Two model programs have been developed for preservice and inservice training of teachers in the instructional applications of computers. The preservice model features a background in computer science, foundations of instructional computing, using a total school view and content specific view; a task-centered practicum in instructional computing; and practice teaching. The inservice training model consists of three stages: (1) initial literacy, (2) implementation, and (3) maintenance or growth. Curriculum maps are provided for both programs, and three references are listed.

Research Studies

This section is not devoted to pure research. If a reading laboratory is loosely defined as a classroom, a document comprised of 10 case studies of the use of microcomputers in reading laboratories could logically be placed in the "Classroom Applications" section. It could also be placed in the "Philosophy" section if it leaned heavily on "why" these micros should be placed this way or in the ";Research Studies" section if the document detailed the growth in reading scores through the use of the microcomputer. A research study or state-of-the-art review might also fall into the "Philosophy" section if the study is liberally interspersed with personal opinion.

Documents in this section take a look at possible health hazards of using computers, CAI and CMI developments in the United States and Canada, studies on teacher and student attitudes toward computers, studies on the use of micros with special student populations, and much more.

JOURNAL ARTICLES

370. Are Computers Hazardous to Your Child's Health? *Personal Computing*. v5, n5, p34–35, 95, May 1981.

The effect of long-term computer use is explored. The effects of radiation and possible damage to the eyes are considered. The author concludes that safety and comfort should play a part in the purchase of computers.

371. CAI Developments in Canada. Hunka, Steve. *Technological Horizons in Education*. v8, n1, p57–59, Jan 1981 (EJ 252 816; Reprint: UMI).

Provides an overview of the use of computers in education in Canada, focusing on the application of microcomputers in elementary and secondary education. Also examines mini- and large-scale systems at institutional and industrial levels.

372. Changes in Attitudes of Preservice Special Educators toward Computers. Vensel, George J. *Teacher Education and Special Education*. v4, n3, p40–43, Sum 1981.

Twenty-three preservice special education teachers were not generally favorable to the prospect of using computers in the classroom, but a demonstration of a microcomputer system produced a large shift in their attitudes.

373. Classroom Computers: Do They Make a Difference? Spencer, Mima; Baskin, Linda. *Classroom Computer News*. v2, n2, p12–15, Nov-Dec 1981.

This research review indicates what is currently known and not known about microcomputers in computer assisted instruction for grades K-12.

374. A Comparison of the Problem Solving Styles of Two Students Learning Logo: A Computer Language for Children. Watt, Daniel H. *Creative Computing*. v5, n12, p86–88, 90, Dec 1979 (EJ 213 419; Reprint: UMI).

An 18-month study of an elementary school computer laboratory is discussed using a case study of two sixth-grade students.

375. Computer Assisted Instruction with Learning Disabled Students. Watkins, Marley W.; Webb, Cynthia. *Educational Computer Magazine*. v1, n3, p24–27, Sep-Oct 1981 (Available from P.O. Box 535, Cupertino, CA 95015.

After reviewing previous findings on the effectiveness of CAI, the authors report on a study in which 28 learning disabled elementary students received math instruction on Apple microcomputers, while matched controls received traditional special education.

376. Computerized Reading Instruction: A Review. Mason, George E. *Educational Technology*. v20, n10, 18–22, Oct 1980 (EJ 234 640; Reprint: UMI).

Discusses some of the more familiar computer assisted instruction systems (such as PLATO, TICCIT, Stanford, and PLAN), including their knowledge base, market sources, and adaptation in college, elementary, and secondary education reading programs. Microcomputer based CAI is mentioned briefly.

377. Computer Literacy in the High School. Thomas, Rex A. *AEDS Journal*. v9, n3, 71–77, Spr 1976.

Describes an instrument created to measure the general level of computer literacy of high school students and to obtain baseline data on student awareness of computer concepts.

378. Computer Literacy, School Mathematics and Problem Solving: Three for the Price of One. Bell, Frederick H. *AEDS Journal*. v12, n4, p163–70, Sum 1979 (EJ 209 481; Reprint: UMI).

Incorporating computers and computing into high school mathematics courses and college teacher education courses had no negative effects on students' achievement levels and attitudes toward mathematics. Instead, it had a positive effect on their attitudes toward computers.

379. The Current Status of Computer Literacy: NAEP Results for Secondary Students. Carpenter, Thomas P., et al. *Mathematics Teacher*. v73, n9, p669–73, Dec 1980 (EJ 237 482; Reprint: UMI).

Data on computer literacy from the 1977-78 National Assessment of Educational Progress (NAEP) are discussed.

380. Educational Technology Research: Computer-Aided Learning of a Foreign Vocabulary. Engel, F. L.; Andriessen, J. J. *Educational Technology*. v21, n5, p46–53, May 1981 (EJ 247 472; Reprint: UMI).

Two experiments assessed individual and group response to using a microcomputer for vocabulary improvement in Dutch-to-English instruction. Findings indicate that a compromise has to be found between using a straightforward learning aid, such as a microcomputer, and a more general purpose instructional system, with additional facilities like sound and graphics.

381. Insights from a Microcomputer Center in a Rural School District. Joiner, Lee Marvin, et al. *Educational Technology*. v20, n5, p36–40, May1980 (EJ 228 295; Reprint: UMI).

Describes an in-house project run by students and local school staff to study the feasibility of using microcomputers for school management, computer assisted instruction, computer literacy, computer programing, and community services. Hardware tests, hardware problems, and rationale for system choice are also discussed.

382. Into the Electronic Learning Era: Implications for Education and Psychological Research: An Interview with Mary Alice White. *Educational Technology*. v21, n9, p9–13, Sep 1981.

Dr. Mary Alice White, a leading researcher on the effects of television on children, describes the new age of electronic learning and discusses what we know and do not know about how children learn from electronic media.

383. Market Accelerates for Educational Microcomputers. *Personal Computing*. v5, n2, p11–12, Feb 1981.

An overview of a study that analyzes and forecasts issues and trends for microcomputers at all educational levels is presented. More information is available from Creative Strategies International, 4340 Stevens Creek Boulevard, Suite 275, San Jose, CA 95129.

384. The Media Specialist and the Computer: An Analysis of a Profession's Attitude towards a New Technology. Smeltzer, Dennis K. *Technological Horizons in Education*. v8, n1, p50–53, Jan 1981 (EJ 252 814; Reprint: UMI).

Reports the results of a survey given to members of the Texas Association for Educational Technology (N=29), in which media specialists' attitudes toward computers and use of computers in society and education were assessed. Results indicate positive attitudes of media specialists toward the role of computers.

385. The Microcomputer as a Multi-user Interactive Instructional System. Jelden, D.L. *AEDS Journal*. v14, n4, p108–217, Sum 1981.

Reports on a four-year study of CAI in which microcomputers were used in individual college classrooms as interactive instructional systems. Discusses students' feelings about CAI, the computer hardware and software, and the lesson models involved.

386. Microcomputers and Education: Planning for the Coming Revolution in the Classroom. Dickerson, Laurel; Pritchard, William H., Jr. *Educational Technology*. v21, n1, p7–12, Jan 1981 (EJ 240 911; Reprint: UMI).

Reasons for the general lack of active planning for a programmatic approach to this new technology are presented, gaps in current microcomputer use are identified, and data collected from public school districts in Florida are analyzed.

387. Microcomputers and Hyperactive Children. Kleiman, Glenn, et al. *Creative Computing*. v7, n3, p93–94, Mar 1981 (EJ 244 588; Reprint: UMI).

Presents research designed to find ways to capitalize on the potential benefits of computers for hyperactive and attention-deficient children. The results indicated that children did almost twice as many problems on the computer as they did with paper and pencil.

388. Microcomputers Are Motivating. Cox, Dorothy; Berger, Carl F. *Science and Children*. v19, n1, p28–29, Sep 1981 (EJ 251 547; Reprint: UMI).

Reports results of a study examining the effectiveness of microcomputers as aids in developing problem-solving skills. Group dynamics of students working with microcomputers was also explored, as well as the effectiveness of this instructional aid with students of varying abilities.

389. Microcomputers in the Classroom: A Foot in the Door. Bolton, Harold; Mosow, David K. *Educational Computer Magazine*. v1, n3, p34–36, Sep-Oct 1981 (Available from P.O. Box 535, Cupertino, CA 95015).

To study attitudes toward computer assisted instruction in social studies, secondary students and teachers in Mobile, Alabama were asked to use the microcomputer based simulation "Civil War." Pre- and postassessment scores of subjects' knowledge and attitudes concerning microcomputers are discussed.

390. Microcomputer Software Development for Schools: What, Who, How? Blaschke, Charles L. *Educational Technology*. v19, n10, p26–28, Oct 1979 (EJ 214 694; Reprint: UMI).

Presents a survey of user needs for microcomputer software in elementary and secondary schools. Approaches to software development are highlighted, and the future of microcomputers is discussed.

391. Off to a Good Start with Microcomputers. Cunningham, Sandra. *Educational Computer Magazine.* v1, n3, p38–39, Sep-Oct 1981 (Also available from P.O. Box 535, Cupertino, CA 95015).

In 1980–81, 10 microcomputers were introduced into seven elementary schools and one junior high school in Hinsdale, Illinois. This article reports a survey of 22 educators' reactions, perceptions, and needs in relation to the new microcomputer program.

392. Research: One Computer Literacy Skill. Guthrie, John T. *Journal of Reading.* v24, n5, p458–60, Feb 1981.

Describes a research project which attempted to sketch the pattern of interaction between a person and a computer terminal. Implications for educators are drawn.

393. A Study of Computer Impact on Society and Computer Literacy Courses and Materials. Austing, Richard H. *Journal of Educational Technology Systems.* v7, n3, p267–74, 1978–79.

This description of a project to review computer impact on society and computer literacy courses and materials includes the effort to gather and maintain a comprehensive bibliography, an analysis of the literature currently included, a set of objectives for courses, and future plans for refinement.

394. Toward Defining the Role of CAI: A Review. Dence, Marie. *Educational Technology.* v20, n11, p50–54, Nov 1980.

The author suggests that CAI is not being used as widely or as effectively as it might be if more educators were familiar with its capabilities. She reviews the research on CAI.

395. USC Study Assesses Micros' Future. Lundell, Allan. *InfoWorld.* v3, n4, p38–39, May 11 1981.

Presents some conclusions of a recently completed two-year study conducted at the University of Southern California.

396. What Teachers Think Every High School Graduate Should Know about Computers. Hansen, Thomas P., et al. *School Science and Mathematics.* v8, n6, p467–72, Oct 1981 (EJ 252 772; Reprint: UMI).

Presents a study which measured secondary school mathematics and science teachers' (N=3576) opinions on what students should know about computers.

MICROFICHE

397. AI Based Personal Learning Environments: Directions for Long Term Research. AI Memo 384. Goldstein, Ira P.; Miller, Mark L., Massachusetts Institute of Technology, Cambridge, MA. Artificial Intelligence Laboratory, Dec 1976, 37p. Sponsoring Agency: National Science Foundation, Washington, DC (ED 207 580; Reprint: EDRS).

The application of artificial intelligence (AI) techniques to the design of personal learning environments is an enterprise of both theoretical and practical interest. In the short term, the process of developing and testing intelligent tutoring programs serves as a new experimental vehicle for exploring alternative cognitive and pedagogical theories. In the long term, such programs should supplement the educational supervision and guidance provided by teachers. This paper illustrates the long-term perspective with a scenario using Sherlock, a hypothetical LOGO tutoring system for elementary graphics programing, which was in a preliminary design state at the time this paper was written. Twenty-three references are listed.

398. Assessment and Documentation of a Children's Computer Laboratory. AI Memo 460. Massachusetts Institute of Technology, Cambridge, MA. Artificial Intelligence Laboratory, Sep 1977, 28p. Sponsoring Agency: National Science Foundation, Washington, DC (ED 207 589; Reprint: EDRS).

The proposed research will thoroughly document the experiences of a small number of fifth-grade children in an elementary school computer laboratory using LOGO, an advanced computer language designed for children. This documentation of a LOGO learning experience will offer specific information about the use of current advanced educational technology in an elementary school classroom, pinpoint the skills and knowledge acquired by the students, and provide evidence about the possible transfer of learning into more general cognitive skills, such as problem solving. The information and methodologies tested will point out possibilities for large-scale verification of the observed gains, as well as provide the basis for practical curriculum development. The information provided will also help form a basis for the decisions to be made by educators throughout the country in the next few years concerning the use of computational technology in public school classrooms.

399. The Brookline LOGO Project. Final Report. Part II: Project Summary and Data Analysis. AI Memo No. 545. LOGO Memo No. 53. Papert, Seymour, et al. Massachusetts Institute of Technology, Cambridge, MA. Artificial Intelligence Laboratory, Sep 1979, 223p. Sponsoring Agency: National Science Foundation, Washington, DC (ED 196 423; Reprint: EDRS).

During the school year 1977–78, four computers equipped with LOGO and Turtle Graphics were installed in an elementary school in Brookline, Massachusetts. All sixth-grade students in the school had between 20 and 40 hours of hands-on experience with the computers. The work of 16 students, ranging from intellectually gifted and average to learning disabled, was documented in detail. This volume includes: (1) an overview of the Brookline LOGO project; (2) a description of the learning styles of different students who took part in the project; (3) a description of student experiences at both extremes of the range of abilities present in a typical public school; (4) a breakdown of the computer programing skills and concepts learned by the students during the course of the project; (5) a breakdown of the mathematical and geometrical skills and concepts learned by the students during the course of the project; and (6) a description of the results of a brief exposure of students to a dynamic turtle which simulates Newtonian motion. Numerous illustrations are included.

400. The Brookline LOGO Project. Final Report. Part III: Profiles of Individual Students' Work. AI Memo No. 546. LOGO Memo No. 54. Watt, Daniel, Massachusetts Institute of Technology, Cambridge,

MA. Artificial Intelligence Laboratory, Sep 1979, 224p. Sponsoring Agency: National Science Foundation, Washington, DC (ED 196 424; Reprint: EDRS).

During the school year 1977–78, four computers equipped with LOGO and Turtle Graphics were installed in an elementary school in Brookline, Massachusetts. All sixth-grade students in the school had between 20 and 40 hours of hands-on experience with the computers. The work of 16 students, ranging from intellectually gifted and average to learning disabled, was documented in detail. This volume contains 16 separate profiles, written by the classroom teacher, which describe the LOGO experiences of each of the subjects in some detail. Each profile includes a statement of how the child was perceived as a student in the regular academic areas of the school, a description of what the child learned in the LOGO classes, an analysis of each child's particular strengths and problems, and the particular teaching strategies that were considered appropriate for each child. Most of the students' work related to computer graphics, but a few also undertook nongraphics projects. The 16 students represented a wide range in interests, abilities, and cognitive styles.

401. Calculators & Computers in the Classroom. East, Philip; Moursund, David, Oregon State Department of Education, Salem, OR, 1979, 67p (ED 174 456; Reprint: EDRS).

A review of the literature on the use of calculators and computers in instruction is presented. Topics covered include: (1) statements of goals for the instructional use of calculators and computers; (2) position statements; (3) supply and demand for computer resources; (4) a technical overview; (5) calculators in elementary schools; (6) computers in high school education; (7) computer science courses for teachers; (8) a selection of articles from the Oregon Council for Computer Education; (9) a review of *Creative Computing* magazine; (10) a listing of information sources.

402. A Case Study of a Young Child Doing Turtle Graphs in LOGO. AI Memo 375. Solomon, Cynthia J.; Papert, Seymour, Massachusetts Institute of Technology, Cambridge, MA. Artificial Intelligence Laboratory, Jul 1976, 10p. Sponsoring Agency: National Institute of Education (DHEW), Washington, DC: National Science Foundation, Washington, DC (ED 207 578; Reprint: EDRS).

This paper describes and comments on a seven year old's experiences with Turtle Graphics, in order to explore some important issues with regard to using computers in education and to probe into the question of what programing ideas and projects will engage young children. The case study which is described took place at the Artificial Intelligence LOGO Laboratory at the Massachusetts Institute of Technology, where the child, a second grader, spent several hours on a consecutive Saturday and Sunday talking in LOGO to a display turtle and a PD-11/45 computer and engaging in debugging sessions. Nine references are listed.

403. Computer Assisted Learning in U.S. Secondary/Elementary Schools. Chambers, Jack A.; Bork, Alfred, Association for Computing Machinery, New York, NY, Jul 1980, 50p (ED 202 461; Reprint: EDRS).

A sample of 974 school districts was surveyed by mail to determine the current and projected use of computers in United States public secondary and elementary schools, with special reference to computer assisted learning. Returned questionnaires provided a 62.3 percent response rate and were balanced both geographically and by urban/rural distribution. Analyses indicated that 90 percent of the districts were currently using the computer, with projections to 94 percent by 1985. Instructional usage was reported by 74 percent, with projections to 87 percent by 1985. A total of 54 percent of the districts reported use of the computer for computer assisted learning, with projections to 74 percent by 1985. Major usage is in secondary schools for drill and practice in mathematics, natural sciences, business, and language arts. Projections for 1980-85, however, indicate greater usage in the social sciences at the secondary levels, as well as growth at the elementary school levels in all subject areas. Projections also indicate shifts to tutorials and simulations, with microcomputers as the delivery systems. Major impediments to usage were identified as lack of money, lack of knowledge about computer assisted learning and computers in general, faculty attitudes, and the need for more and better computer assisted learning modules.

404. Computer Supported Instruction in California Elementary and Secondary Schools. A Status Report. Stutzman, Carl R. Mar 1981, 39p. Paper presented at the Annual Fresno Research Symposium (2nd, Fresno, CA, Apr 24, 1981) (ED 206 304; Reprint: EDRS).

A survey instrument was sent to the superintendent of each school district in California in June 1980 to gather information about the uses of computers in instruction in the state's public elementary and secondary schools. The findings of the study indicate that: (1) just over one-third of the districts use computers in instruction; (2) at least two-thirds of the computer using districts use microcomputers; (3) hands-on experience in 82 percent of computer using districts is limited to less than 25 percent of the students; (4) mathematics, followed by computer science/literacy, business education, and career education is the most popular curricular application; (5) BASIC is used in over 60 percent of the instructional applications; (6) over 60 percent of the teachers in districts using computers are either unprepared or inadequately prepared to function in a computer supported environment; and (7) one-third of the districts not using computers are planning to initiate a program next year or soon after.

405. Contributions of Cognitive Science and Related Research on Learning to the Design of Computer Literacy Curricula. Report No. 81-1. Series in Learning and Cognition. Mayer, Richard E., California University, Santa Barbara, CA. Department of Psychology, Dec 1980, 35p. Sponsoring Agency: National Institute of Education (DHEW), Washington, DC (ED 203 551; Reprint: EDRS).

A review of the research on techniques for increasing the novice's understanding of computers and computer programing considers the potential usefulness of five tentative recommendations pertinent to the design of computer literacy curricula: (1) provide the learner with a concrete model of the computer; (2) encourage the learner to actively restate the new technical information in his/her own words; (3) assess the learner's existing intuitions about computer operation and try to build on or modify them; (4) provide the learner with methods for chunking statements into smaller, meaningful parts; and (5) provide the learner with methods for analyzing statements into smaller, meaningful parts.

Concludes that, while results of cognitive research provide qualified support for the first two recommendations, more active research is needed on the other three. A bibliography lists 59 references, and appendices include seven statements used in a BASIC-like instructional booklet. Examples of six types of test problems for a BASIC-like language, an example of an elaboration exercise, and data from a study in the review are also included.

406. The Development and Implementation of a District Education Program. Final Report. Walzl, F. Neil, Newark School District, DE, Nov 1975, 395p. EdD Practicum, Nova University, Fort Lauderdale, FL. Not available in hard copy due to marginal reproducibility of original (ED 126 934; Reprint: EDRS).

The goal of a district computer education program at Glasgow High School, Newark, Delaware, was to model full utilization of computer services in a public high school. The phases of the project included: (1) development of goals and objectives at the district level; (2) workshops for teacher training; (3) minicourses for students; (4) developing courses for the 1975–76 school year; and (5) establishing a long-range computer services plan for the district. This report discusses the historical development of the project, summarizes events in each phrase, and provides results of an evaluation, including numerous documents and exhibits illustrating the activities which took place during the project.

407. Development of an Index of Computer Anxiety. Rohner, Daniel J.; Simonson, Michael R. Apr 1981, 37p. Paper presented at the Annual Convention of the Association for Educational Communications and Technology (Philadelphia, PA, Apr 6–10, 1981). Not available separately; available as part of ED 207 487 (ED 207 487; Reprint: EDRS).

This paper discusses the need for a measure of computer anxiety and describes the development of an index, consisting of 10 target statements and 20 distractor statements, which was administered during the fall of 1980 to 175 education students in the undergraduate media course at Iowa State University. The score from the 10 target items were correlated to sex, hemisphericity, and field dependence. An analysis of variance was calculated between the scores on the Computer Anxiety Index and the subject's college major. While no statistically significant relationships were found for any variable, there appeared to be a slight relationship between hemisphericity and computer anxiety. The Computer Anxiety Index reliability estimate was fairly high ($r = .86$), but there is a question of whether it is a valid measurement of ''intent to use'' the computer in the classroom. Further research on computer anxiety is recommended, and a list of 25 references is provided, as well as sample pages from the index.

408. Early Adolescent Use of Selected Problem-Solving Skills Using Microcomputers. Cox, Dorothy Anna Howard. 1980, 264p. Ph.D. Dissertation, University of Michigan, Ann Arbor, MI (ED 200 449; Reprint: EDRS).

Reports on a study that examined an evaluation of the characteristics, interactions, problem-solving strategies, and achievement of seventh- and eighth-grade junior high school students ($N=66$) as they interacted with a microcomputer in three problem solving sessions. Study also looked at a determination of the effectiveness of three original microcomputer programs, using topics from life science, social studies and environmental science in problem solving, and a fourth program in specific skill training in organizing data using a matrix. Selected conclusions indicate that: (1) students can improve in problem-solving skills in a short time on a microcomputer; (2) the training session in organizing data into a matrix was successful in introducing a usable new strategy; (3) individuals worked better in teams than alone; (4) subjects were just as motivated when sessions were more infrequent; (5) influence of group interaction enabled subjects of all abilities to successfully participate in and solve problems; (6) all subjects adapted easily and quickly to the use of a microcomputer; (7) subject interest remained high, regardless of achievement or variances of individual characteristics; and (8) microcomputers can be considered a viable, motivating aid for the development of some problem-solving skills of early adolescents.

409. Educational Computing in the Northwest, 1979: Status, and Needs for Information and Assistance. Edwards, Judith B., Northwest Regional Educational Laboratory, Portland, OR, Jun 1979, 54p. Sponsoring Agency: National Institute of Education (DHEW), Washington, DC (ED 201 308; Reprint: EDRS).

Two surveys were conducted by the Computer Technology Program of the Northwest Regional Educational Laboratory in the spring of 1979 to obtain information for planning a clearinghouse of computer based educational materials and a regional program of user support and technical assistance. A postcard questionnaire was sent to all school superintendents in the six states in the region to determine the current status and future plans for computer use in administration and instruction.

A more comprehensive study of information and assistance needs was conducted through a survey of teachers who were at least somewhat knowledgeable of or experienced with using computers in instruction. The questionnaire for teachers was composed of six sections: demographic data, computer use, ways of meeting current information and assistance needs, software sources, information needs, and assistance needs. The results of the two surveys are reported with 17 supporting tables. The conclusions include a discussion of availability of computer terminals, uses of computers, current ways of meeting information and assistance needs, and needs for information and assistance. A sample questionnaire and cover letter from each survey are appended.

410. Educational Implications of In-Home Electronic Technology. Research Memorandum—33. Walling, Victor C., Jr., et al., SRI International, Menlo Park, CA, May 1979, 72p (ED 188 600; Reprint: EDRS).

This study identifies and assesses the potential impact of new electronic technologies on education in private homes and looks beyond immediate incremental changes to broader, more subtle, complex, or threatening changes that may require attention from federal policymakers. Some educational implications are discussed: (1) equality of access to high-quality education, including opportunity for the disadvantaged and handicapped; (2) the organization of education in society, including local school finance, private schools, alternative education, and national education resources; and (3) the federal role, with sections discussing monitoring and research, planning and policymaking, and support for capacity building. The appendices provide discussions of the in-home educational needs of poor and low-motivated students and the handicapped, trends in developing and marketing new technology with in-home educational potential, and current federal activities related to in-home educational technology.

411. The Effects of Learning a Computer Programming Language on the Logical Reasoning of School Children. Seidman, Robert H. Apr 14, 1981, 63p. Paper presented at the Annual Meeting of the American Educational Research Association (Los Angeles, CA, Apr 14, 1981) (ED 25 206; Reprint: EDRS).

The research reported in this paper explores the syntactical and semantic link between computer programing statements and logical principles and addresses the effects of learning a programing language on logical reasoning ability. Fifth-grade students in a public school in Syracuse, New York were randomly selected as subjects and then randomly placed in either the experimental or the control group. The experimental group was taught LOGO, a programing language developed for use with young children. The control group received no special instruction. At the end of the treatment period, both groups were administered a series of tests measuring their conditional reasoning abilities. Tests were scored in two distinct ways; the two groups were statistically compared within both scoring schemes by split-plot two-factor repeated measures and one-way analysis of variance. Students in the experimental group who interpreted conditional logic statements biconditionally performed significantly better on the inversion fallacy principle than the control group; no significant difference was found when test items were scored in the traditional manner. Comparison of pre- and postexperiment achievement test scores showed a significant improvement in reading only for the control group. Some areas for further research are suggested and a 64-item bibliography is attached.

412. An Evaluation of the Costs of Computer-Assisted Instruction. Program Report No. 80-B7. Levin, Henry M.; Woo, Louis, Stanford University, Stanford, CA. Institute for Research on Educational Finance and Governance, May 1980, 38p. Sponsoring Agency: National Institute of Education (DHEW), Washington, DC (ED 198 794; Reprint: EDRS).

Cost data were collected from a study on the effectiveness of using CAI for culturally disadvantaged children in the Los Angeles Unified School District. Based on the resource ingredients approach to measuring costs, it was found that up to three daily 10-minute sessions of drill and practice could be provided for each child within the present allocation of funds from Title I of the Elementary and Secondary Education Act of 1965. If the computer system were shared between two schools, the higher costs would permit only two daily sessions. Costs were also estimated for a more advanced CAI system and were found to be in the same range, probably because the costs of software do not decline with more advanced technology.

413. Exploring the Microcomputer Learning Environment. Independent Research and Development Project Reports. Report #5. Loop, Liza; Christensen, Paul, Far West Laboratory for Educational Research and Development, San Francisco, CA, Nov 1980, 90p (ED 201 307; Reprint: EDRS).

The current state of the art on the educational use of microcomputers is explored through a review of the literature and through observations and interviews with teachers and practitioners. A working taxonomy to characterize typical computer augmented learning environments (CALEs) was developed, which consisted of environmental elements, activity segments, teacher-learner environment situations, and learner attributes. Results of the interviews with teachers and practitioners showed that, in their CALEs, teachers concentrated less on the presentation of curriculum context and more on computer literacy, thinking and problem skills, and computer applications. Their expressed needs were for more computers, quality software, and computer related CALEs include: (1) the "hardware reliability" problem; (2) the "access" problem; (3) the "friendly environment" problem; (4) the "social pressure" problem; and (5) the "overbearing person" problem. A hierarchy of achievement that most students pass through was specified, which included fear, curiosity, understanding, and tool use. The profile of a successful computer student showed that such learners tended to be bright, math- and science-oriented, logical or analytical thinkers, persevering, and male. Details on the survey itself and the taxonomy are appended. Extensive references are provided.

414. Extending a Powerful Idea. Artificial Intelligence Memo No. 590. Lawler, Robert W., Massachusetts Institute of Technology, Cambridge, MA. Artificial Intelligence Laboratory, Jul 1980, 22p. Sponsoring Agency: National Science Foundation, Washington, DC (ED 207 804; Reprint: EDRS; also available from Artificial Intelligence Laboratory, 545 Technology Square, Room 338, Cambridge, MA 02139).

This document focuses on the use of a computer and the LOGO programing language by an eight-year-old boy. The stepping of variables, which is the development and incrementally changing of one of several variables, is an idea that is followed in one child's mind as he effectively directs himself in a freely chosen, problem-solving situation. The specific case of this child is used to show how the power of the computer in education can go well beyond the "traditional" roles of drill and practice and game playing.

415. Instructional Computing in Wyoming: Status and Recommendations. Kansky, Bob, Wyoming University, Laramie, WY. Science and Mathematics Teaching Center, 1981, 51p. Sponsoring Agency: Wyoming University, Laramie, WY, Center for Research Services and Publications (ED 202 675; Reprint: EDRS).

The status of instructional computing in Wyoming's public schools as of April 1980 is reported. Specifically, the document indicates the nature and extent of computer usage in grades K-12 and summarizes teachers' opinions regarding the potential instructional uses of computers in the schools. Presents the recommendations of a select committee of Wyoming educators with respect to the statewide development of instructional applications of computers.

416. Instructional Computing: Ten Case Studies. Hargan, Carol; Hunter, Beverly, Human Resources Research Organization, Alexandria, VA, 1978, 245p. Sponsoring Agency: National Science Foundation, Washington, DC. Directorate for Science Education. (ED 166 018; Reprint: EDRS).

These case studies are written for educational institutions that wish to plan, extend, or improve their use of computers for learning and teaching. Each case study includes a brief description of the profile of the institution; history of the development of instructional computing; organization and management; student access to computing; cost and budgeting; student accomplishments; spectrum of applications; computer literacy; computer science; outreach; plans and goals; lessons learned; contracts; and references.

417. Issues Related to the Implementation of Computer Technology in Schools: A Cross-Sectional Study. Children's Electronic Laboratory Memo No. 1. Sheingold, Karen, Bank Street College of Education, New York, NY, Feb 19, 1981, 19p. Sponsoring Agency: National Institute of Education (DHEW), Washington, DC (ED 205 165; Reprint: EDRS).

Three school systems were examined to assess issues pertinent to microcomputer innovations in the schools and to determine whether a revolution in education was taking place because of this new technology. A case study approach was used in this exploratory analysis in order to collect information from four sources: students, administrators, technology specialists, and the community. The three sites chosen for the study were selected on the basis of the diversity of their geographic location and the type of school population served. It was discovered that school systems tend to adapt microcomputer use to their own goals, needs, and ways of operating. Although several common trends were observed among the systems studied, it was concluded that microcomputers on their own will not promote any particular outcomes and their impact will depend largely on the educational context in which they are embedded. A paucity of research literature on the educational and developmental consequences for children using microcomputers is indicated.

418. The Microcomputer as an Interactive Instruction System in the Classroom. Jelden, David L., University of Northern Colorado, Greeley, CO, 1980, 248p (ED 194 710; Reprint: EDRS).

A study was conducted from March 1976 through June 1980 on the application and feasibility of a computer micro system as an interactive tutorial instructional tool in a self-contained classroom. Literature on CAI, hardware, and software was examined. Individualized CAI materials for industrial arts and technology electronics were generated. An instructional model and guidelines for its use were developed. Microprocessor system instructional effectiveness and human factors associated with its classroom use were examined.

Findings include the following: (1) CAI program generation is possible only if instructors develop instructional units which stand alone, yet interrelate with each other; (2) instructors must consider individual student differences and use student feedback extensively; (3) computers purchased for CAI use should be standard, meet certain minimum capacity requirements, and have readily available maintenance services; (4) most students found CAI as good or better than other media in teaching concepts and skills, felt CAI helped them better meet course objectives and found lessons readable and easily understood; and (5) CAI lessons showed a positive correlation to student grades.

Findings affirm CAI feasibility. Investigation of microcomputers for simulation purposes or for use by the handicapped are recommended. A 100-page appendix contains CAI sample "coursewriter," computer programs, evaluation forms, course outlines, a pretest, list of microcomputer suppliers by product/system, and a bibliography.

419. Microcomputers in Alberta Schools. Final Report. Petruk, Milton W., Alberta Department of Education, Edmonton, AB, Canada. Planning and Research Branch, Feb 1981, 43p (ED 205 214; Reprint: EDRS).

Data for this study, which was conducted to provide a status report describing the nature and extent to which microcomputers have been introduced into schools in Alberta, Canada were collected through two-phase mail survey. Results showed that nearly 12 percent of the schools now have one or more microcomputers. The majority of the units are Commodore PET (45 percent), Apple II (31 percent), and Radio Shack TRS-80 (19 percent); they appear to be uniformly distributed across all grade levels. The most frequently reported uses of the microcomputer involved the teaching of computer literacy and computer assisted instruction. The majority of microcomputer users expressed the need for additional equipment, software, and training. While a relatively small number reported that they had no interest in introducing microcomputers into their schools, the majority that do not have a microcomputer are anticipating getting one or more in the future. However, a large proportion of this group felt that they did not know enough about microcomputers to anticipate what their needs might be. The remainder tended to report a strong need for information about both equipment and programs and a strong need for additional training. Copies of the questionnaires used are appended.

420. Microcomputers in Library Automation. Simpson, George A., MITRE Corporation, McLean, VA, Dec 1978, 56p. Sponsoring Agency: Office of Education (DHEW), Washington, DC (ED 174 217; Reprint: EDRS).

As librarians cope with reduced budgets, decreased staff, and increased demands for services, microcomputers will take a significant role in library automation by providing low-cost systems, solving specific library problems, and performing in distributed systems. This report presents an introduction to the technology of this low-cost, miniature computer and a descripion of its specific applications in libraries. The use of such computers in circulation, acquisition, serials control, reference, administration, and audiovisual services is covered. Current and probable future uses of the microcomputer in each of these areas are described. References are listed at the end of each chapter, and appendices provide glossaries of computer and library terms and a list of vendors supplying automated library systems.

421. Preschool Children Use Apple II to Test Reading Skills Programs. Piestrup, Ann McCormick, Advanced Learning Technology, Portola Valley, CA, Jan 28, 1981, 13p (ED 202 476; Reprint: EDRS).

Fifty-five three and four year olds used an Apple II microcomputer to learn reading readiness concepts of "above," "below," "left," and "right." Available during indoor play periods for three weeks at a nursery school on the Stanford University campus, the microcomputer was accepted enthusiastically by children, teachers, and parents as an activity center; criterion tests on the four reading skill concepts showed that children improved after the three-week period with the microcomputer. Color graphics, music, and voice response to keyboard inputs by the children were elements used in the program, and children evidenced considerable enjoyment using the computer. While the Apple was monitored at all times by a research assistant, the children soon learned how to operate it properly and how to take care of both the microcomputer and the diskettes used to run the program.

422. Results of Computer Assisted Instruction at Bath Elementary School. Martha Holden Jennings Foundation, Cleveland, OH, 1979, 26p. Parts may be marginally legible (ED 195 245; Reprint: EDRS).

This pilot project at Bath Elementary School in Richfield, Ohio was conducted to assess the feasibility of CAI for the Revere Local Elementary Schools. The primary focus of the project was to assist sixth-grade students in using the computer as an interactive instructional system in the areas of remedial reading, mathematics, and vocabulary. All 100 sixth-grade students used the computer daily for a school semester for either remediation or enrichment. Preliminary data showed that students gained an average of 2.4 months in reading proficiency during the months they used the computer, and academic gains were reported to be higher for those students who used CAI. The project report includes a sample of a student computer survey and a parent computer survey, work and sign-up schedules used during the pilot program, and newspaper/newsletter reports on the project.

423. Shall We Teach Structured Programming to Children? LaFrance, Jacques E., 1979, 11p (ED 192 767; Reprint: EDRS).

To study the effectiveness and feasibility of using structured programing games at the elementary school level, this study presented one and one-half hours of programing instruction to a group of gifted children between the ages of 9 and 12. Using a game called "Antfarm" and the programing language Pascal, the instruction introduced certain structured programing features, such as basic commands, concepts of sequence, iteration, selection and refinement, and the notion of hierarchical structure. Results showed high motivation for the entire group. A few children were beginning to use top-down design, to define their own modules, and to give them names. Two problems noted were that the selection commands were difficult for the children to learn, and technical bugs sometimes caused the program to abort. A 19-item bibliography is attached.

424. A Study of Computer Use and Literacy in Science Education. Final Report, 1978–1980. Klassen, Daniel L., et al., Minnesota Educational Computing Consortium, Saint Paul, MN, 1980, 208p. Not available in hard copy due to marginal legibility of original document. Appendices A, C, and G removed due to copyright restrictions. Appendix F missing from document prior to its being shipped to EDRS for filming. Sponsoring Agency: National Science Foundation, Washington, DC (ED 191 712; Reprint: EDRS).

This research project was designed to provide information which will be of assistance to science educators responsible for and interested in the development, implementation, and evaluation of educational programs and courses designed to foster computer literacy. A questionnaire concerning computer use in the classroom was answered by 3,576 science teachers. The data from the questionnaire demonstrated that teachers strongly support minimal understanding of computers and their societal role for every secondary school student and that they generally feel positive about the value of computers in education. Responses of the 929 students who had been exposed to instructional computing activities demonstrated significant gains in both affective and cognitive dimensions of computer literacy.

425. A Technology Assessment of Personal Computers. Vol. I: Summary. Nilles, Jack M., University of Southern California, Los Angeles, CA. Office of Interdisciplinary Program Development, 1980, 79p. Sponsoring Agency: National Science Foundation, Washington, DC (ED 202 452; Reprint: EDRS).

This volume summarizes the results of a two-year technology assessment of personal computers. The purpose of this study was to explore possible future modes of growth of the personal computer and related industries, to assess the impacts and consequences of that growth, and to present some of the policy issues and options which may arise as a consequence of the development of personal computer technology. However, due to limitations of time, funds, and personpower, detailed analyses were restricted to three main issue areas: (1) the growth of personal computer technology; (2) the expected impacts of the technology; and (3) the public policy implications in areas of education, employment, and international trade. Much of the information generated in this report was based upon the results of Delphi surveys. Tables of data are included.

426. A Technology Assessment of Personal Computers. Vol. II: Personal Computer Technology, Users, and Uses. Nilles, Jack M., University of Southern California, Los Angeles, CA. Office of Interdisciplinary Program Development, Sep 1980, 121p. Sponsoring Agency: National Science Foundation, Washington, DC (ED 202 453; Reprint: EDRS).

This volume reports on the initial phase of a technology assessment of personal computers. First, technological developments that will influence the rate of diffusion of personal computer technology among the general populace are examined. Then, the probable market for personal computers is estimated and analyzed on a functional basis, segregating it into four submarkets: the home, education, small business, and large organizations. Next, some possible evolutionary forms of the personal computer are briefly described, along with an alternative mode of development of personal computing. In conducting this phase of the assessment, the researchers used a survey of existing personal computer users and market growth models for large-ticket consumer durable goods to predict the probable growth and maturation patterns of the personal computer market. Tables of data are included, as well as an extensive bibliography.

427. A Technology Assessment of Personal Computers. Vol. III: Personal Computer Impacts and Policy Issues. Nilles, Jack M., et al., University of Southern California, Los Angeles, CA. Office of Interdisciplinary Program Development, Sep 1980, 342p. Sponsoring Agency: National Science Foundation, Washington, DC (ED 202 454; Reprint: EDRS).

A technology assessment of personal computers was conducted to study both the socially desirable and undesirable impacts of this new technology in three main areas: education, employment, and international trade. Information gleaned from this study was then used to generate suggestions for public policy options which could influence these impacts. Four primary methods were used to develop the information for the policy analysis stages of the assessment: (1) search and analysis of the relevant literature; (2) development of a series of scenarios of alternative futures; (3) performance of two Delphi surveys and a cross-impact analysis based on these scenarios, and (4) interviews and/or surveys of the potentially affected stakeholders and decisionmakers. Tables of data are included, as well as a list of references. Appendices include Delphi questionnaires, with summaries of findings and an employment questionnaire used in the study.

428. Towards More Effective Teaching and Learning: New Directions for Educational Technologies in the 1980s—Research and Studies. Botkin, James W., et al., International Center for Integrative Studies, New York, NY, Sep 15 1980, 77p. Contains occasional light and broken type. Sponsoring Agency: Horace Mann Learning Center (ED), Washington, DC (ED 200 403; Reprint: EDRS).

The significance of innovations in educational technology is examined. Issues such as measuring effectiveness and analyzing costs and the impact of these issues on classrooms, schools, and whole systems of education are discussed. A listing of current projects, with summaries, is provided.

429. Use of Computers for Instructional Purposes in Ontario Schools. Lawton, Stephen B.; McLean, Robert S., Aug 1980, 34p. Sponsoring Agency: Ontario Institute for Studies in Education, Toronto, ON, Canada (ED 207 152; Reprint: EDRS).

A survey undertaken in June 1980 sought to determine the types of computers used for instructional purposes in the Ontario schools. A brief questionnaire was sent to elementary and secondary schools, both public and private. The study revealed that the present use of computers in instruction is confined almost exclusively to secondary schools. Seventy-four percent of the responding secondary schools reported using computers for instructional purposes, although the percentage varies widely by region. Use of computers is highest in the most populous regions and is also related to school enrollment. The elementary schools reported using only microcomputers, but at the secondary level, all types of computers proved popular. A primary recommendation of the study is the establishment of more uniform access to computers in secondary schools. Decisions about the type of computer provided must be based upon individual schools' needs and resources. Appended are a sample questionnaire and tables presenting survey results.

430. The Use of Microcomputers for Training: Business and Industry. Kearsley, Greg, et al., Human Resources Research Organization, Alexandria, VA, Mar 1981, 10p (ED 207 598; Reprint: EDRS).

Training directors or managers of 160 major corporations of the ''Fortune 500'' were surveyed to assess the scope of computer use in the training domain; information was received from 56 of the companies. The study focused on five major areas: training applications, hardware, software, courseware, and number of students involved. An analysis of the data collected indicates that: (1) the use of computer based training (CBT) is becoming more commonplace in business and industry; (2) technical skills and management training are the most common uses; (3) the APPLE II is the most prevalent microcomputer in use; (4) software/courseware is primar-

ily internally developed; (5) simulation is the most common instructional strategy used; (6) many of the efforts involve large numbers of employees; and (7) some companies are adopting a phased approach to the integration of CBT. Examples of microcomputer based training projects in several corporations are described. Future prospects in microcomputer based training are also discussed, e.g., the use of videodisc, videotext and videoconferencing services, and embedded training. Seven references are listed.

431. The Use of Microcomputers in a Communication Network. Underwood, Barry, ed., Computer Using Educators of B.C., Campbell River, BC, Canada, May 1981, 77p. Best copy available. Sponsoring Agency: Educational Research Institute of British Columbia, Vancouver, BC, Canada (ED 208 850; Reprint: EDRS).

This study examines how the microcomputer could be used in a network with other microcomputers, some established computer technology, and the most recent developments in communication technology. It was also intended to provide information on the feasibility of a provincial communication network between the schools of British Columbia, Canada. It was anticipated that, with such a network in place, a teacher consultation service between schools could be established and the exchange of quality instructional software packages facilitated. The project consisted of an examination of the communication possibilities between two microcomputers, a mainframe, a community bulletin board system, a database (electronic library), and a knowledge network. The results were that, after a number of physical connection difficulties, it was possible to use the microcomputer in the conditions under which it was tested. However, high transmission costs were a limiting factor on such a network because of the slow speed of transmission and the current lack of multiple users. A 29-item bibliography is included.

432. Using PLATO to Teach Problem Solving. Steinberg, Esther, R., Illinois University, Urbana, IL. Computer-Based Education Research Laboratory, Aug 1980, 65p. Sponsoring Agency: National Institute of Child Health and Human Development (NIH), Bethesda, MD (ED 202 455; Reprint: EDRS).

This report describes the results of three studies which investigated the use of PLATO to teach problem solving. Subjects were 244 children from kindergarten through third grade. The first study explored the extent to which kindergartners and second graders used the knowledge about which answers were right and which were wrong to develop the correct strategy to solve a novel picture problem. The next study looked at the procedures used by kindergartners and second graders while they were in the process of trying to get the answer. The third study considered three methods of teaching problem-solving skills to first and third graders: experience only; visual feedback; and interactive instructional feedback on problems done incorrectly. Abstracts, methods, results, and discussions are given for each of the studies. Results of this research led to a post hoc study, which is described. Seven figures show sample displays and nine references are also given.

Home Computers

Originally, there was not going to be a section on the home computer in this resource guide because what, after all, does the home computer have to do with formal education? As it turns out, home computers may have a great deal to do with formal education.

Interspersed throughout the literature on microcomputers are occasional vignettes: the first-grade student who refused to use the teacher's dittoed material for math drill and practice because he was accustomed to using his computer at home; the young child who was unintentionally threatening to the teacher because she knew far more about computers than the teacher; a comparison of today's home without a computer to yesterday's home without books and the development of a class of information poor or illiterate people. Yes, indeed, the home computer is having an impact on formal education.

The references in this chapter range from a two-page philosophical look at the impact of home computers to the 350-page reference book on how, where, and why to select a home computer.

JOURNAL ARTICLE

433. A Computer Revolution? Cole, Phyllis. *People's Computers.* v6, n4, p8–11, Jan–Feb 1978.

A future is postulated in which the consumer can buy a small home computer to perform a variety of functions, such as regulating heating, lighting, smoke alarms, burglar alarms, and providing video entertainment. Improved computer languages will be needed and are likely to be developed in the near future.

BOOKS

434. The Home Computer Revolution. Nelson, Theodor H. South Bend, IN: The Distributors, 1977, 224p.

Written in a chatty, readable style, this book provides an overview of the birth of the computer and how the world is going to be changed by it. The author attempts to demystify computer technology and describes many uses for the home computer.

435. Home Computers Can Make You Rich. Weisbecker, Joe. Rochelle Park, NJ: Hayden Book Company, Inc., 1980, 122p.

This book assumes some familiarity with computers but suggests some references for the novice. The premise of the book is that home computers are here to stay and that one might as well put his/her hobby to good use—and make money. The book is divided into 11 chapters: (1) "The Microcomputer Industry"; (2) "What You Need to Know about Making Money"; (3) "Resources You Can Use"; (4) "Choosing Your Hardware"; (5) Writing for Money"; (6) Creating and Selling Programs"; (7) "Services for Sale"; (8) Use Your Imagination"; (9) "Invent Your Way to Success"; (10) "Making Your Money Grow"; and (11) "Working at Home.

436. 1001 Things to Do with Your Personal Computer. Sawusch, Mark. Blue Ridge Summit, PA: Tab Books, 1980, 335p.

The purpose of this book is to provide a plethora of applications of interest to the microcomputer owner, to discuss and briefly illustrate how to create the software for the applications, and to spawn ideas for other personal computer applications for the reader. It includes: (1) "Applications for Everyone"; (2) "Business and Financial Applications"; (3) "Mathematical Applications"; (4) Technical and Scientific Applications"; (5) "Educational Applications"; (6) Hobby Applications"; (7) "Game and Recreational Applications"; (8) "Control and Peripheral Applications"; (9) "Artificial Intelligence and the Future Personal Computer"; (10) "Utility Programs"; (11) "Miscellaneous"; and (12) "A Compendium of Additional Applications." It is not just a "how-to-do-it" book but a "what-to-do" book as well.

437. Owning Your Home Computer. Perry, Robert L. New York: Everest House, 1980, 224p.

The author introduces home computers to the reader and explains how to understand, select, and use the home computer for business, entertainment, and education functions. A glossary of terms is included, along with a listing of over 1,000 computer programs now available on the general market. Chapter nine lists 99 common functions of a home computer.

438. Peanut Butter & Jelly Guide to Computers. Willis, Jerry W. Portland, OR: Delithium Press, 1978, 207p.

This book is designed to be a simple, easy-to-digest source of information on personal computing. It begins with a bit of history and continues on to provide the reader with computer terminology and enough information to get started in the home computing game.

439. A Simple Guide to Home Computers. Ditlea, Steve, New York: A & W Visual Library, 1979, 220p.

This book is a simple introduction to the world of home computers. It examines the background of home computers, describes the workings and basic operations of the home computer, discusses how to evaluate system capabilities with an eye to selection, and tells the home computer owner what s/he might expect once the computer is installed in the home. A glossary is included.

440. Why Do You Need a Personal Computer? Levanthal, Lance A.; Stafford, Irvin. New York: John Wiley & Sons, Inc., 1981, 278p.

This book discusses personal computers from the point of view of the potential user. It describes how ordinary people can use personal computers; compares different types of computers; discusses the requirements for a useful computer; introduces the BASIC computer language; describes the problems involved in writing programs; describes peripherals and interfacing; discusses the operation and maintenance of computers and peripherals; and discusses the selection of a computer.

References/Resources

Almost every document in this resource guide is a resource of some kind, but this section focuses on the following: (1) guides which lead the reader to additional resources; (2) guides which are complete in and of themselves; (3) bibliographies; (4) compendiums of facts and tips regarding microcomputers; (5) glossaries; (6) sources of state and federal support for micro hardware and software; (7) sources of local funds or local support for obtaining micros; (8) directories of computer using schools and colleges; and (10) book reviews and more.

JOURNAL ARTICLES

441. A Beginner's Guide to Memory. Hughes, Elizabeth M. *onComputing*. v3, n1, p18–26, Sum 1981 (EJ 245 099; Reprint: UMI).

This article is designed to equip the reader with the information needed to deal with questions of computer memory. Discusses core memory; semiconductor memory; size of memory; expanding memory; charge-coupled device memories; magnetic bubble memory; and read-only and read-mostly memories.

442. A Beginner's Guide to Microcomputer Resources. Goldberg, Albert L. *Audiovisual Instruction*. v24, n8, p22–23, Nov 1979 (EJ 214 647; Reprint: UMI).

Presents a compilation of books, journals, and newletters related to microcomputers and a list of manufacturers of microcomputers.

443. Classroom Computer News. Prentice, Lloyd; Beckelman, Laurie. *Instructor*. v91, n3, p85–90, 94, 96–98 Oct 1981 (EJ 250 729; Reprint: UMI).

The editors of *Classroom Computer News* prepared this compendium of news and tips for using computers in the classroom. Topics include computer literacy, the benefits of classroom computer use, ways of programing IEPs, courseware selection, the basics of microprocessors, and new products.

444. Computer Literacy Bibliography. Friel, Susan; Roberts, Nancy. *Creative Computing*. v6, n9, p92–97, Sep 1980 (EJ 232 840; Reprint: UMI).

This annotated bibliography is an alphabetized listing of current resources on computers under the following topics: computer applications/societal issues; programing, computer definition of a computer; teaching resources; and periodicals. Publications are coded for elementary, junior high, senior high, and reference usage.

445. Computer Literacy—Finding Effective Resources. Kurshan, Barbara. *Recreational Computing*. v9, n4, p45–47, Jan–Feb 1981.

The author presents an annotated bibliography of instructional resources—including texts, films, journals, and children's books—about computers.

446. Computer Literacy: Sounds Scary, But Getting Started Is Easy! Best, Anita. *The Computing Teacher*. v7, n2, p14–17, Oct–Nov 1979.

Presents teachers with some practical ideas on computer instructional literacy resources and introductory teaching activities.

447. Computers and Computer Resources. Bitter, Gary. *Teacher*. v97, n5, p62–63, Feb 1980 (EJ 226 891; Reprint: UMI).

This resource directory provides brief evaluative descriptions of six popular home computers and lists selected sources of educational software, computer books, and magazines.

448. Designing Good Educational Software. Kingman, James C. *Creative Computing.* v7, n10, p72, 74, 76, 78, 80–81, Oct 1981 (EJ 252 711; Reprint: UMI).

A random sampling of computer software designed for educational use is reviewed.

449. ERIC/RCS: Computer Literacy, Part I: An Overview. O'Donnell, Holly. *The Reading Teacher.* v35, n4, p490–94, Jan 1982.

Several ERIC resources on computers in education are reviewed in this article.

450. Finding Funds for Microcomputers. Pathe, Kenton; Ernst, Mary. *American School and University.* v54, n4, p22–25, Dec 1981.

Suggests sources of federal, state, and local funds for hardware purchase and software development.

451. Kids for Computers. Walker, Alan B. *Compute!* v3, n1, p28, 30–31, Jan 1981.

Explains how a fifth-grade class raised money to buy microcomputers for their school.

452. Learning with Micros. Frenzel, Louis E. *Interface Age.* v6, n7, p34, Jul 1981.

Presents a list, with addresses and brief annotations, of some noteworthy publications in the field of computer technology.

453. Lightening the Load with Computer-Managed Instruction. Hedges, William. *Classroom Computer News.* v1, n6, p34, Jul–Aug 1981.

Briefly defines computer managed instruction, lists criteria for good CMI programs, and provides the addresses of major producers of CMI packages.

454. Microcomputers and Education. Lopez, Antonio M., Jr. *Creative Computing.* v7, n3, p140–43, Mar 1981 (EJ 244 593; Reprint: UMI).

A directory of resources related to computers lists magazines and newsletters; sources of information; university educators involved in microcomputing; others involved in microcomputer education; and some sources of educational software. Also included is a list of articles on computers in education, alphabetized by author.

455. Microcomputer Software for Instructional Use: Where Are the Critical Reviews? Lathrop, Ann. *The Computing Teacher.* v9, n6, p22–26, Feb 1982.

This article lists journals and newsletters which regularly include instructional software reviews and describes the type of review offered by each. Reviews include software for the Apple, PET, TRS-80, and Atari systems, unless otherwise noted.

456. Microcomputers: Step 1. Sullivan, Ada. *Early Years.* v12, n2, p36, 65, Oct 1981.

Presents a brief microcomputer glossary for teachers.

457. Microelectronics and Music Education. Hotstetter, Fred T. *Music Educators Journal.* v65, n8, p38–45, Apr 1979 (EJ 215 482; Reprint: UMI).

This look at the impact of microelectronics on CAI in music notes trends toward new applications and lower costs. Includes a rationale for CAI in music; a list of sample programs; comparison of five microelectronic music systems; PLATO cost projections; and sources of further information.

458. Raising Money for Technology: Some Do-it-Yourself Ideas. Sturdivant, Patricia. *Electronic Learning.* v1, n1, p22, 24, Sep–Oct 1981.

Presents ideas for obtaining funds for electronic learning aids.

459. Resources Are Macro for Micros. *Instructional Innovator.* v25, n6, p29–31 Sep 1980 (EJ 232 617; Reprint: UMI).

Lists names and addresses of some manufacturers, software distributors, magazines, and book publishers specializing in commercial resources for microcomputers.

460. A School Computer. Yours for the Asking. McCable, Jim. *Creative Computing.* v6, n9, p48, 50, 52–53, Sep 1980.

A computer hobbyist describes his campaign to acquire donated microcomputer equipment for his daughter's elementary school.

461. Securing Local Support for Your Computer Project. Roecks, Alan L. *Educational Technology.* v19, n7, p16–18, Jul 1979 (EJ 206 860; Reprint: UMI).

Guidelines for securing and maintaining local funding for computer related projects include suggestions in the areas of establishing and maintaining project/school board relationships; encountering social and political obstacles; and defining guidelines for project implementation. Successes and failures of the MICA project are provided as illustrations.

462. Special-Interest Microcomputing Publications. Colsher, William L. *onComputing.* v2, n2, p60–64, 66–67, Fall 1980 (EJ 229 352; Reprint: UMI).

This article describes computer journals, newsletters, and cassette magazines that are devoted to a particular brand of personal computer, such as the TRS-80, or to a particular microprocessor, such as the 6502, used in the Apple II, Commodore PET, and other microcomputers. Publishers' addresses and rates are listed.

463. Ten Tips for Home Computer Care and Repair. Shapiro, Neil. *Popular Mechanics.* v155, n4, p112–15, Apr 1982.

The author asserts that there are some repairs to both the computer and its assorted attachments that can be done by the layperson.

464. What Did You Do in Computer Class? Lee, Thé. *Personal Computing.* v5, n7, p44–45, 47–48, 50–51, 54–55, Sep 1981.

This article is intended as an activist parent's guide for getting computers into the schools. The grassroots program in Cupertino, California is described as an example.

MICROFICHE

465. Academic Computing Directory. A Search for Exemplary Institutions Using Computers for Learning and Teaching. Human Resources Research Organization, Alexandria, VA, 1977, 125p. Sponsoring Agency: National Science Foundation, Washington, DC (ED 148 396; Reprint: EDRS).

This directory identifies some of the schools, colleges, and universities that successfully use computers for learning and teaching in the United States. It was compiled to help teachers, administrators, computer center workers, and other educators exchange information, ideas, programs, and courses. Individuals listed as contacts are willing to share their knowledge with others. Ninety-four elementary and secondary schools, 71 public school districts, 37 community colleges, 158 private and public colleges and universities, and 7 public access institutions are listed. Entries are arranged geographically, by state, for each type of the institution and include information on reasons for inclusion, enrollment, users, illustrative applications, computers, terminals, public information, and contact. A list of exemplary institutions in academic computing is attached.

466. Calculators and Computers in the Classroom: Select Summaries of Current Education Topics. Know-Pak No. 17. Moursund, David; East, Phillip, Oregon State Department of Education, Salem, OR, Oct 1979, 27p (ED 191 710; Reprint: EDRS).

The usage and availability of calculators, computers, and related instructional materials are presented. This publication is a "Know-Pak," a summary of materials and articles that is part of a series of information packets developed by the Oregon Department of Education. Topics covered include: (1) a forecast of a computer literacy crisis in American education; (2) model goals for computer education; (3) sample program course and instructional goals; (4) computer use in Oregon; (5) computer and calculator terminology; (6) calculator use in elementary schools; (7) available textbooks; (8) sample problems; and (9) lists of current computer assisted instruction projects.

Annotated bibliographies on articles from the *Oregon Computing Teacher*, selected summarized reports from the Oregon Council for Computer Education, and other sources of information, such as publications, organizations, and people active in Oregon's computer education programs, are also included.

467. Computer-Based Education. The Best of ERIC, June 1976–August 1980. Hall, Keith A., ERIC Clearinghouse on Information Resources, Syracuse, NY, Nov 1980, 96p. Sponsoring Agency: National Institute of Education (DHEW), Washington, DC (ED 195 288; Reprint: EDRS).

This bibliography contains annotations of reports, reviews, conference proceedings, documents, and journal articles on computer based education (CBE). Most of them were derived from a search of the Educational Resources Information Center (ERIC) system. Covering June 1976 through August 1980, this compilation serves as an update to two earlier papers—"The Best of ERIC: Recent Trends in Computer Assisted Instruction" (1973) and "Computer Assisted Instruction: The Best of ERIC 1973-May 1976." A brief introduction discusses instructional methods included in computer based education and explains the subject headings used in the bibliography: (1) historical references; (2) new technology, such as artificial intelligence and videodiscs; (3) new audiences, such as off-campus, handicapped, or incarcerated learners; (4) various content area applications, including such fields as English, health sciences, languages and social studies; (5) developmental efforts, such as PLATO, TICCIT, and others concerned with teacher training; (6) basic research in computer assisted instruction; and (7) conference proceedings on computers in education. An author index is included, as well as information for ordering ERIC documents.

468. Computer Literacy. Rosen, Elizabeth; Hicks, Bruce, Illinois University, Urbana, IL. Department of Secondary Education, Jun 1977, 10p. Illinois Series on Educational Applications of Computers (ED 142 200; Reprint: EDRS).

Briefly reviews informational books dealing with simple concepts and terminology related to computers. Recommendations are made as to those which are better for children and high school students. A bibliography lists all books considered.

469. Computers in the Secondary Mathematics Curriculum. Copple, Christine. Jun 1981, 34p (ED 204 144; Reprint: EDRS).

The purpose of this document is to increase the educator's awareness of the present status of computers in the school. Although the study was directed at computers in the secondary mathematics curriculum, much of the material dealt with broader aspects of the computer in all secondary curricula. The first section of this report consists of a glossary of commonly used computer oriented terms. The bulk of the document is a series of annotations of some of the current literature on computers. The first portion focuses on facts, figures, positions, and attitudes regarding computer use in the secondary curriculum. The second set of annotations deals with computer uses in the mathematics classroom and is subdivided into the following areas of concentration: (1) the teaching of computer literacy; (2) the teaching of computer science; and (3) computer assisted instruction. The final annotation section focuses on the special aspects of microcomputers. The document concludes with a summary, some general conclusions, and two specific recommendations regarding computer use at the secondary level.

470. A General Introduction to Microcomputers. Muiznieks, Viktors, Illinois University, Urbana, IL. Department of Secondary Education, Nov 1978, 19p. Illinois Series on Educational Applications of Computers, No. 26 (ED 178 054; Reprint: EDRS).

This basic introduction to microcomputers provides the neophyte with the terminology, definitions, and concepts that explain the microcomputer and computing technology in general. Mathematical operations with binary numbers, computer storage, controlling logic, and the concepts of stack and interrupt are explained.

471. Guide to Microcomputers. Frederick, Franz J., Association for Educational Communications and Technology, Washington, DC; ERIC Clearinghouse on Information Resources, Syracuse, NY, 1980, 159p. Sponsoring Agency: National Institute of Education (DHEW), Washington, DC (ED 192 818; Reprint: EDRS; also available from AECT Publications Sales, 1126 16th Street, NW, Washington, DC 20036).

This comprehensive guide to microcomputers and their role in education discusses the general nature of microcomputers; computer languages in simple English; operating systems and what they can do; compatible systems; special accessories; service and maintenance; computer assisted instruction, computer managed instruction and computer graphics; time-sharing and resource-sharing; potential instructional and media center applications; and special applications, e.g., electronic mail, networks, and videodiscs. Available resources are presented in a bibliography of magazines and journals about microcomputers and software and their uses; a selected list of companies specializing in creating specialized languages and applications programs for microcomputers; and a selected list of companies specializing in the preparation of educational programs for use on microcomputers.

472. Microcomputers in Education: Applications of Microprocessors in the Schools. A Report to the Northeast Regional Education Planning Project. Tinker, Robert; Naiman, Adeline, Technical Education Research Center, Cambridge, MA, May 15 1980, 100p (ED 196 455; Reprint: EDRS; also available from Technical Education Research Centers, 8 Eliot Street, Cambridge, MA 02138).

The three-month study of the role of microcomputers in schools described in this report focuses on the six New England states and the state of New York. The report covers instructional software available for the most frequently used microprocessors, including samples from several regions. It examines production of a resource listing of instructional courseware according to computer type, program language, grade level, objectives of the instructional program, location, cost, and source. (See appendices for software bibliography.) It gives examples of current school applications and the roles of microprocessors within the seven participating states and identifies at least 10 locations where schools have successfully integrated the use of "personal computers" in the K-12 curriculum. The report goes on to identify policies or program procedures being used by various states to control or assist in the purchase of hardware and relates the development of a databank of educational software and user evaluations of software on a commercial time-shared system. Included in the appendices are a software bibliography, a description of hardware available to schools, sample programs, addresses of organizations concerned with microcomputers and education, state survey reports, and program listings.

473. Reference Manual for the Instructional Use of Microcomputers. Volume I (Release II). Forman, Denyse, et al., JEM Research, Victoria, BC, Canada, 1981, 873p. (ED 208 849; Reprint: EDRS; also available from JEM Research, Discovery Park, P.O. Box 1700, Victoria, BC V8W 2Y2, Canada).

This manual is intended to provide educators with information and guidelines for locating, selecting, and purchasing commercially available courseware for the Apple II microcomputer. A courseware index is provided which lists programs in broad subject areas and grade levels. Information given for each program includes its DOS, language, cost, publisher, and distributor, as well as a short description. This index can be used to locate commercially available programs in a particular subject area and for a specific grade level. Catalogs from 63 publishers and producers of microcomputer courseware are included, as well as an alphabetized list of the addresses of over 200 publishers, distributors, and manufacturers of computer products. An annotated bibliography of microcomputer journals, magazines, and newsletters provides descriptions of the publications; the addresses and yearly subscription rates; and comments on the general usefulness of the publications. A list of selected compatible accessories and expansion options for the Apple II is also provided.

474. School Microware: A Directory of Educational Software. Over 500 Programs/Packages for APPLE, PET, TRS-80. Dresden Associates, Dresden, ME, Sep 1980, 52p (ED 196 431; Reprint: EDRS; also available from Dresden Associates, P.O. Box 246, Dresden, ME 04342).

This preliminary directory represents the offerings of 45 software suppliers and gives information about instructional software currently available for three microcomputers widely used in schools. It is geared toward a wide variety of users, including school planners contemplating microcomputer acquisition; teachers planning courses and curricula; media center personnel; schools of education; and home computer users. The directory is organized as follows: (1) software descriptions in sequence by school department, subject, and lowest grade level; (2) summary listings of software for individual hardware systems, in the same sequence as the first section; (3) an alphabetical listing of software suppliers and their addresses; and (4) a glossary of terms used. Software descriptions include the program name, department, subject, grade level range, program type, and functional description, as well as intended hardware system(s), source, and retail price. The summary listing contains only the program name, grade level range, functional description, and an identification number which refers back to the more complete entry in the first section.

BOOKS

475. The Complete Microcomputer System Handbook. Safford, Edward L., Jr. Blue Ridge Summit, PA: Tab Books, 1979, 322p.

Written in a lighthearted manner, this book is designed for the layperson. It is divided into 11 chapters: (1) "Calculators and Common Sense"; (2) "Computer Comparison and How Computers Operate"; (3) "Making Computers Run and Analyzing Their Output"; (4) Input Data and More on Programming"; (5) "What is a Program and Let's Examine Some"; (6) "Computer Problems and Troubles"; (7) "Computer Tests and Test Equipment"; (8) "Computers in Networks"; (9) "Computerized Decision Making"; (10) "Computers and Robots"; and (11) "Magnetic Bubble Memories and Other Concepts."

476. The First Book of Microcomputers. Moody, Robert. Rochelle Park, NJ: Hayden Book Company, Inc, 1978, 139p.

In this book, segments of computing are broken down into easily understood blocks. Included are a glossary, written in layperson's terms and accompanied by cartoons and "interviews" with computers; a discussion of what makes a computer work; and answers to the most-asked questions. The book concludes with a review of the more popular periodicals treating home computing and a list of computer stores and computer clubs.

477. **Free-Lance Software Publishing: The First Concise Step-by-Step Guide to Selling Your Own Computer Programs.** Korites, B. J. Littleton, MA: Kern Publications, 1979, 133p.

This publication is designed to provide accurate and authoritative information on writing and selling computer programs. It describes, in detail, the six basic methods of selling software. They are: by direct sale; in book form; through intermediaries; through service bureaus; through private tapes; and through user's groups. Also covered are marketing; selling; contract negotiations (sample contract is included); pricing; writing the user's manual; and, in the case of large-computer software, installation and maintenance.

478. **Microcomputers and the 3 r's: A Guide for Teachers.** Doerr, Christine. Rochelle Park, NJ: Hayden Book Company, Inc., 1979, 177p.

Written for teachers with limited knowledge of computers, this book consists of three main sections: (1) a nontechnical discussion on microcomputers, their history, and capabilities and a summary and discussion of the benefits of using computers in the classroom; (2) an overview of the wide range of educational computer use, with a chapter on each of the major types of instructional applications, including computer science, problem solving, simulations, games, and computer assisted instruction and simple administrative applications; and (3) instructional computing resources (organizations and publications) and information on computer products available today, along with a discussion of the advantages of certain features.

479. **1979-80 Microcomputer Report of the Minnesota Education Computing Consortium.** Minnesota Educational Computing Consortium (MECC), Lauderdale, MN: MECC Instructional Services Division, 1979–80, 88p.

This report provides pertinent information about existing microcomputer hardware; pertinent information about instructional use of microcomputers; and information for the MECC and the national educational community on the potential for use of microcomputers. Information sheets used for the microcomputer study are included.

Appendix:
Additional Sources of Information

Interest in microcomputers is at an all-time high. A few believe that the micro craze is a flash-in-the-pan phenomenon which will fade. Evidence abounds, however, to refute this. New computer journals are proliferating; groups are forming around the nation whose sole purpose is to exchange computer tips, techniques, and news; national educational associations are forming subgroups whose sole purpose is to investigate the uses of computers in education; and textbook publishers are rushing into the computer software development race. This appendix is designed to round out this resource guide by providing information on locating computer journals; catalogs and directories; user groups; associations; computer science degrees; microcomputer centers to visit; and software sources.

COMPUTER JOURNALS

AEDS Journal and AEDS Monitor
Association for Educational Data Systems
1201 16th St., N.W.
Washington, DC 20036

Frequency: quarterly
Focus: administrative applications and instructional design

Byte
70 Main St.
Peterborough, NH 03458

Frequency: monthly
Focus: technical home computers

Classroom Computer News
Intentional Educations, Inc.
51 Spring St.
Watertown, MA 02172

Frequency: bimonthy
Focus: classroom and administrative applications; hardware, software, and book reviews; and annotated bibliographies

The Computing Teacher
Department of Computer and Information Science
University of Oregon
Eugene, OR 97403

Frequency: monthly
Focus: classroom applications; teacher education; software and book reviews

Creative Computing
P.O. Box 789-M
Morristown, NJ 07960

Frequency: monthly
Focus: classroom applications; software reviews; programing techniques

Educational Computer Magazine
P.O. Box 535
Cupertino, CA 95015

Frequency: bimonthly
Focus: some classroom applications; home computer use; software and book reviews; computer conference calendar

Educational Computing
MAGSUB (Subscription Services) Ltd.
Oakfield House, Perrymount Road
Haywards Heath, Sussex RH16 3DH England

Frequency: monthly
Focus: classroom applications; new products

Educational Technology
140 Sylvan Ave.
Englewood Cliffs, NJ 07632

Frequency: monthly
Focus: classroom applications; software, books, and product reviews

80 Microcomputing
P.O. Box 997
Farmingdale, NY 11737

Frequency: monthly
Focus: some classroom applications; home computers

Electronic Education
Electronic Communications, Inc.
1311 Executive Center Dr., Suite 220
Tallahassee, FL 32301

Frequency: 10 each year
Focus: classroom applications; hardware and software reviews

Electronic Learning
Scholastic Inc.
902 Sylvan Ave., Box 2001
Englewood Cliffs, NJ 07632

Frequency: bimonthly
Focus: classroom applications; software reviews; evaluation of
  commercial programs; guides to proposal writing and funding

Journal of Educational Technology Systems
Baywood Publishing Company, Inc.
120 Marine St., Box D
Farmingdale, NY 11735

Frequency: quarterly
Focus: technical curriculum development

Mathematics Teacher
National Council of Teachers of Mathematics
1906 Association Dr.
Reston, VA 22091

Frequency: monthly
Focus: classroom applications, with a focus on mathematics;
  software reviews

Personal Computing
P.O. Box 1408
Riverton, NJ 08077

Frequency: monthly
Focus: home computers; business applications; hardware;
  programing

Popular Computing (formerly onComputing)
70 Main St.
Peterborough, NH 03458

Frequency: monthly
Focus: home computers; small business computers

T.H.E. Journal
P.O. Box 992
Acton, MA 01720

Frequency: 6 per year
Focus: software and project reviews; theoretical and technical
  approaches

CATALOGS AND DIRECTORIES

Classroom Computer News. v1, n6, Jul–Aug 1981.

Practical Guide to Computers in Education. Coburn, Peter,
et al. Reading, MA: Addison-Wesley Publishing Company,
1982, 266p.

USER GROUPS

Alaska Association for Computers in Education (AACE)
The Northern Institute
650 W. International Airport Rd.
Anchorage, AK 99502

Alberta Association for Educational Data Systems
838 Education Tower, University of Calgary
2500 University Dr., N.W.
Calgary, AB T2N 1N4 Canada

Apple for the Teacher
5848 Riddio St.
Citrus Heights, CA 95610

Boston Computer Society
Educational Resource Exchange
3 Center Plaza
Boston, MA 02108

Computer Education Resource Coalition (CERC)
Lesley College
29 Everett St.
Cambridge, MA 02238

Computer Education Society of Ireland
Mount Anville Secondary School, Goatstown
Dublin 14, Ireland

Computers, Learners, Users, Educators Association
  (CLUES)
50 Nellis Dr.
Wayne, NJ 07470

Computer-Using Educators (CUE)
Independence High School
1776 Educational Park Dr.
San Jose, CA 95133

DECUS
1 Iron Way
Marlboro, MA 01752

DIDACOM
Avenbeech 98, 2182 RZ Hillegom
The Netherlands

Educational Computing Consortium of Ohio
4777 Farnhurst Rd.
Cleveland, OH 44124

Educational Computing Organization of Ontario (ECOO)
252 Bloor St., West
Toronto, ON M5S 1V6 Canada

Educators Interest Group of the San Diego Computer Society
P.O. Box 81537
San Diego, CA 92138

Illinois Association for Educational Data Systems (ILAEDS)
Computer Science Department
Northern Illinois University
De Kalb, IL 60115

Indiana Computer Educators
Fort Wayne Community Schools
1230 S. Clinton St.
Fort Wayne, IN 46802

Manitoba Association for Educational Data Systems
(MAN-AEDS)
Neepawa Area Collegiate, Box 430
Neepawa, MB ROJ 1HO Canada

Michigan Association for Computer Users in Learning
(MACUL)
c/o Wayne County Intermediate School District
33500 Van Born Rd.
Wayne, MI 48184

Minnesota Association for Educational Data Systems
1925 W. Country Rd. B2
Saint Paul, MN 55113

New Hampshire Association for Computer Education
Statewide (NHACES)
University of New Hampshire, Computer Services
Durham, NH 03824

Northwest Council for Computers in Education
Computer Center, Eastern Oregon State College
La Grande, OR 97850

Saskatchewan Association for Computers in Education
Mount Royal Collegiate, 2220 Rusholme Rd.
Saskatoon, SK S7L 4A4 Canada

The Science Teachers' Association of Ontario
306 Beulea Dr.
Nepean, ON K2G 4A8 Canada

Society of Data Educators (SDE)
983 Fair Meadow Rd.
Memphis, TN 38117

Texas Computer Education Association
7131 Midbury
Dallas, TX 75230

The Utah Council for Computers in Education
1295 N. 1200 West
Mapleton, UT 84663

West Australian Computer Educators
12 Lilac Pl., Dianella, 6062
Western Australia

Wyoming Educational Computing Council
Laramie County School District 1
Administration Building, 2810 House Ave.
Cheyenne, WY 82001

ASSOCIATIONS

American Association of School Administrators (AASA)
1801 N. Moore St.
Arlington, VA 22209

Computer related activities: holds conferences; supports administrative applications of the computer
Publications: *The School Administrator*

American Educational Research Association (AERA)
1126 16th St., N.W.
Washington, DC 20046

Computer related activities: holds conferences; exchanges research on the university level; maintains interest in computer assisted instruction
Publications: *American Educational Research Journal; Educational Evaluation and Policy; Education Research;* and *Review of Educational Research*

Association for Computers in Mathematics and Science
Teaching
P.O. Box 4
Austin, TX 78765

Computer related activities: exists as a professional organization for college mathematics and science teachers
Publications: *Journal of Computers in Mathematics and Science Teaching*

Association for Computing Machinery (ACM)
1133 Avenue of the Americas
New York, NY 10036

Computer related activities: maintains special interest groups on all areas of computing
Publications: *The ACM Guide to Computer Science and Computer Applications Literature; Communications;* and *Computing Reviews*

Association for Educational Communications and
Technology (AECT)
1126 16th St., N.W.
Washington, DC 20036

Computer related activities: organizes media professionals; maintains special task force on microcomputers
Publications: *Educational Communication and Technology; Instructional Innovator;* and *Journal of Instructional Development*

Association for Educational Data Systems (AEDS)
1201 16th St., N.W.
Washington, DC 20036

Computer related activities: supports administrative applications of computers; serves data processing professionals
Publications: *AEDS Bulletin; AEDS Journal;* and *AEDS Monitor*

Association for the Development of Computer-Based Instructional Systems (ADCIS)
Bond Hall, Western Washington University Computer
  Center
Bellingham, WA 98225

Computer related activities: provides communication links between
  product developers and users; maintains special interest groups
Publications: *ADCIS Newsletter; The Journal of Computer-Based
  Instruction*

International Council for Computers in Education (ICCE)
Department of Computer and Information Science
University of Oregon
Eugene, OR 97403

Computer related activities: exists as a professional organization to
  support classroom applications of computers
Publications: *The Computing Teacher*

Library and Information Technology Association (LITA)
American Library Association
50 E. Huron St.,
Chicago, IL 60611

Computer related activities: supports library automation
Publications: *Journal of Library Automation; LITA Newsletter*

National Association of Secondary School Principals
  (NASSP)
1904 Association Dr.
Reston, VA 22091

Computer related activities: establishes institutes on computers in
  education
Publications: *Curriculum Report; Legal Memorandum; NASSP
  Bulletin;* and *NASSP Newsleader*

National Council of Social Studies (NCSS)
3615 Wisconsin Ave., N.W.
Washington, DC 20016

Computer related activities: exists as a professional organization to
  support classroom applications
Publications: *Social Education*

National Council of Teachers of English (NCTE)
111 Kenyon Rd.
Urbana, IL 61801

Computer related activities: maintains a committee on instructional
  technology, focusing on English and language arts
Publications: *College English; English Journal;* and *Language Arts*

National Council of Teachers of Mathematics
1906 Association Dr.
Reston, VA 22091

Computer related activities: supports classroom applications; es-
  tablishes guidelines for software evaluation
Publications: *Arithmetic Teacher; Journal for Research in
  Mathematics Education; Mathematics Student; Mathematics
  Teacher;* and *NCTM Newsletter*

National Science Teachers Association (NSTA)
1742 Connecticut Ave., N.W.
Washington, DC 20009

Computer related activities: exists as a professional organization for
  secondary school science educators; develops software for energy and interdisciplinary education
Publications: *Journal of College Science Teaching; Science and
  Children; The Science Teacher*

EDUCATION-RELATED

Computer Science Degrees (full degree programs only):

Columbia University
Teachers College
525 W. 120th St.
New York, NY 10027

Fairfield University
Fairfield, CT 06430

Lehigh University
School of Education
524 Brodhead Ave.
Bethlehem, PA 18015

Lesley College Graduate School
29 Everett St.
Cambridge, MA 02238

Nova University
Office of New Programs
3301 College Ave.
Fort Lauderdale, FL 33314

Stanford University
School of Education
Stanford, CA 94305

State University of New York at Stony Brook
Nicholls Road
Stony Brook, NY 11794

University of Florida
College of Education
Gainesville, FL 32611

University of Illinois
Department of Education
1310 S. 6th St.
Champaign, IL 61820

University of Oregon
Department of Computer and Information Science
Eugene, OR 97403

Wayne State University
Detroit, MI 48202

MICROCOMPUTER CENTERS TO VISIT

Math/Computer Education Project
Lawrence Hall of Science
University of California
Berkeley, CA 94720

Purpose: holds workshops for teachers and students; encourages
  class visits

Microcomputer Center
San Mateo Educational Resources Center Library
333 Main St.
Redwood City, CA 94063

Purpose: conducts hands-on workshops for teachers; previews and
  evaluates software; has teacher education classes; promotes
  Softswap exchange, encompassing 200 public domain programs

Microcomputer Resource Center
Teachers College
Columbia University
525 W. 121st St.
New York, NY 10027

Purpose: arranges hands-on workshops for teachers; has print resources; hosts workshops and seminars; evaluates commercial
  computer based curriculum

Minnesota Educational Computing Consortium (MECC)
2520 Broadway Dr.
Saint Paul, MN 55113

Purpose: coordinates state's educational computing system; does
  inservice training; develops curriculum for Apple and Atari

Technical Education Research Centers, Inc. (TERC)
Computer Resource Center
8 Eliot St.
Cambridge, MA 02138

Purpose: conducts workshops; hosts open house on Wednesdays;
  presents hands-on opportunities

SOFTWARE VENDORS

MULTIPLE SYSTEMS:

Activity Resources Inc.
P.O. Box 4875
Hayward, CA 94540
(415) 782-1300

Systems: TRS-80; Apple II
Disciplines: basic math (upper elementary)

Brain Box
601 W. 26th St.
New York, NY 10003
(212) 989-3573

Systems: TRS-80; Apple
Disciplines: reading; English; social studies; American history (upper elementary–high school)

Charles Mann & Associates
55722 Santa Fe Trail
Yucca Valley, CA 92284
(714) 365-9718

Systems: Apple; Texas Instruments; TRS-80
Disciplines: management programs; programs about computers and
  programing (adult)

COMPress
A Division of Science Books International, Inc.
P.O. Box 102
Wentworth, NY 03282
(603) 764-5831

Systems: Apple II; Bell & Howell
Disciplines: chemistry; genetics; statistics; energy; evolution (high
  school–adult)

Compumax, Inc.
P.O. Box 1139
Palo Alto, CA 94301
(415) 321-2881

Systems: Apple; Atari
Disciplines: Lesson writing (adult)

Courseware Magazine
4919 N. Millbrook, #222
Fresno, CA 93726

Systems: PET; Apple; TRS-80
Disciplines: multiple (multiple user levels)

Creative Computing (Sensational Software)
P.O. Box 1139
Morristown, NJ 07960
(800) 631-8112

Systems: Apple; Atari; TRS-80
Disciplines: holdings from MECC and Huntington Computer Project (multiple user levels)

DYNACOMP, Inc.
1427 Monroe Ave.
Rochester, NY 14618
(716) 442-8960

Systems: TRS-80; Apple; Atari; PET; Northstar; CP/M-based
  systems
Disciplines: simple math; word recognition (preschool–primary)

Educational Activities, Inc.
1937 Grand Ave.
Baldwin, NY 11510
(800) 645-3739

Systems: PET; TRS-80 Level II; Apple II Plus
Disciplines: reading; spelling; language arts; math; class management (multiple user levels)

Educational Software Midwest
414 Rosemere Ln.
Maquoketa, IA 52060
(319) 652-2334

Systems: Apple II; Bell & Howell
Disciplines: test construction (adult)

Edu-Soft Steketee Educational Software
4639 Spruce St.
Philadelphia, PA 19139
(215) 747-1284

Systems: Apple II; TRS-80
Disciplines: mathematics

Entelek
P.O. Box 1303
Portsmouth, NH 03801
(603) 436-0439

Systems: Apple; TRS-80; PET; DEC
Disciplines: mathematics; science; graphics; computer language

J. L. Hammett Company, Inc.
Hammett Place
P.O. Box 545
Braintree, MA 02184
(617) 848-1000

Systems: Apple; TRS-80; PET
Disciplines: multiple

K–12 MicroMedia
P.O. Box 17
Valley Cottage, NY 10989
(914) 358-2582

Systems: Apple; Atari; PET; TRS-80
Disciplines: mathematics; language arts; reading; science; computer literacy; social studies; early childhood (K–high school)

Krell Software
21 Millbrook Dr.
Stony Brook, NY 11790
(516) 751-5139

Systems: Apple; PET; TRS-80
Disciplines: SAT preparation programs; LOGO; others

Learning Tools, Inc.
4 Washburn Place
Brookline, MA 02146
(617) 566-7585

Systems: Apple; North Star; Commodore; TRS-80; Texas Instruments; Zenith
Disciplines: curriculum management systems for general and special education; teacher and administrative planning system

McGraw-Hill
1221 Avenue of the Americas
New York, NY 10020
(212) 997-6194

Systems: Apple II; TRS-80
Disciplines: computer literacy; problem solving; geology; history; civics; mathematics (upper elementary)

MECC Publications
2520 Broadway Dr.
Saint Paul, MN 55113
(612) 376-1118

Systems: Apple; Atari
Disciplines: mathematics; language arts; social studies; science (multiple user levels)

Micro Learningware
P.O. Box 2134
North Mankato, MN 56001
(507) 625-2205

Systems: Apple; PET; TRS-80
Disciplines: mathematics; spelling; history; science; business; geology (upper elementary–high school)

Microphys Programs
2048 Ford St.
Brooklyn, NY 11229
(212) 646-0140

Systems: Apple; PET
Disciplines: physics; chemistry; calculus; mathematics; vocabulary; spelling (multiple user levels)

Micro Power & Light
400 108th Ave., N.E.
Bellevue, WA 98004
(206) 454-1315

Systems: Apple; TRS-80
Disciplines: Typing Tutor; mu-Math (upper junior high school–adult)

Program Design, Inc. (PDI)
11 Idar Court
Greenwich, CT 06830
(203) 661-8799

Systems: Apple II; Atari; PET; TRS-80
Disciplines: language arts; programing; mathematics

Quality Education Design
P.O. Box 12486
Portland, OR 97212

Systems: Apple; TRS-80
Disciplines: mathematics (upper elementary)

Random House
High School Division
2970 Brandywine Rd., Suite 201
Atlanta, GA 30341

Systems: Apple II; TRS-80
Disciplines: mathematics; reading; language arts; management
   systems (multiple user levels)

Right On Programs
P.O. Box 977
Huntington, NY 11743

Systems: Apple; PET; TRS-80
Disciplines: mathematics; social studies; science; library programs
   (elementary–junior high school)

Softside
Softside Publications
P.O. Box 68
Milford, NH 03055

Systems: Apple; Atari; TRS-80
Disciplines: multiple (multiple user levels)

Software Exchange
P.O. Box 68
Milford, NH 03055
(603) 673-5144

Systems: Apple; Atari; TRS-80
Disciplines: games (preschool)

Software House, Inc.
695 E. 10th North
Logan, UT 84321
(800) 453-2708

Systems: Apple; Atari
Disciplines: mathematics; games

Teaching Tools: Microcomputer Services
P.O. Box 12679
Research Triangle Park, NC 27709
(919) 851-2374

Systems: Apple; PET; TRS-80
Disciplines: addition; subtraction; spelling; matching games; letters;
   numbers (primary)

VisiCorp
1330 Bordeaux
Sunnyvale, CA 94086
(408) 745-7841

Systems: Apple; Atari; TRS-80
Disciplines: Visi Products

APPLE ONLY:

Addison-Wesley Publishing Company
2725 Sand Hill Rd.
Menlo Park, CA 94025
(415) 854-0300

Disciplines: math games; computer graphing experiments
   (elementary–high school)

Apple Captions
21650 W. Eleven Mile Rd., Suite 103
Southfield, MI 48076
(313) 354-2559

Disciplines: English; math games (primary); study quizzes (upper
   elementary–adult)

Apple Computer, Inc.
10260 Bandley Dr.
Cupertino, CA 94017
(408) 996-1010

Disciplines: mathematics; programing

Avant-Garde Creations
P.O. Box 30161
Eugene, OR 97403
(503) 345-3043

Disciplines: mathematics; physics; chemistry; biology; English;
   German (multiple user levels)

Cook's Computer Company
1905 Bailey Dr.
Marshalltown, IA 50158

Disciplines: mathematics; letter recognition; number recognition;
   art; typing; spelling (primary)

Educational Courseware
3 Nappa Ln.
Les Port, CT 06880
(203) 227-1438

Disciplines: biology; world history; astronomy; physics; population
   studies; test forms (junior high school–adult)

Educational Services Management Corporation
P.O. Box 12599
Research Triangle Park, NC 27709
(919) 781-1500

Disciplines: administrative; special purpose (adult)

Educational Software Professionals, Ltd.
38437 Grand River
Farmington Hills, MI 48018
(313) 477-4470

Disciplines: grammar drills; retail mathematics; educational
   charades; chemistry; test writing (multiple user levels)

Education Programs
Disney Electronics
6153 Fairmont Ave.
San Diego, CA 92120
(714) 281-0285

Disciplines: alphabet drill (preschool); reading; language arts; mathematics (K–junior high school)

Edutek Corp.
P.O. Box 11354
Palo Alto, CA 94306
(415) 325-9965

Disciplines: reading; math games (preschool–elementary)

Edu-Ware Services, Inc.
22222 Sherman Way, Suite 102
Canoga Park, CA 91303
(214) 346-6783

Disciplines: reading; mathematics (multiple user levels)

Hartley Software
P.O. Box 431
Dimondale, MI 48821
(616) 942-8987

Disciplines: reading; language arts; mathematics (K–junior high school)

High Technology Software Products, Inc.
P.O. Box 14665
8001 N. Classen Blvd.
Oklahoma City, OK 73113
(405) 840-9900

Disciplines: administrative; chemistry lab simulations (adult)

Information Unlimited Software, Inc.
281 Arlington Ave.
Berkeley, CA 94707
(415) 525-9452

Disciplines: word processing; data management; mailing programs; Tellstar (adult)

Instant Software
Peterborough, NH 03458
(603) 924-7296

Disciplines: mathematics (elementary)

Instructional Development Systems
29 Virginia Beach Blvd.
Virginia Beach, CA 23452
(804) 340-1977

Disciplines: AIDS (multiple user levels)

MECC Publications
2520 Broadway Dr.
Saint Paul, MN 55113
(612) 376-1118

Disciplines: mathematics; language arts; social studies; science (multiple user levels)

Milliken Publishing Company
Computer Department
1100 Research Blvd.
Saint Louis, MO 63132
(314) 991-4220

Disciplines: mathematics; language arts (multiple user levels)

Milton-Bradley Company
Shaker Road
East Longmeadow, MA 01028
(413) 525-6411

Disciplines: mathematics; language arts (upper elementary)

Monument Computer Service
Village Data Center
P.O. Box 603
Joshua Tree, CA 92252
(800) 854-0561   (800) 432-7257, ext. 802 (California)

Disciplines: administrative (junior high school–high school)

MUSE Software
330 N. Charles St.
Baltimore, MD 21201
(301) 659-7212

Disciplines: mathematics; drawing; speech processing; games (elementary)

Powersoft
P.O. Box 157
Pitman, NJ 08071
(609) 589-5500

Disciplines: engineering; mathematics; statistics (high school–college)

Transnet Corporation
1945 Rt. 22
Union, NJ 07083
(201) 688-7800

Disciplines: multiple packages (multiple user levels)

ATARI ONLY:

Atari, Inc.
1272 Borregas Avenue
Sunnyvale, CA 94086
(408) 745-5069

Disciplines: history; sociology; physics; algebra; spelling; economics (elementary–college)

Santa Cruz Educational Software
5425 Jigger Dr.
Soquel, CA 95073
(408) 476-4901

Disciplines: mathematics; language arts (grades K–high school)

BELL & HOWELL ONLY:

Bell & Howell
7100 N. McCormick Rd.
Chicago, IL 60645
(312) 262-1600

Disciplines: Genis I and PASS authoring languages (adult)

TRS-80 ONLY:

ACORN Software Products, Inc.
634 N. Carolina Ave., S.E.
Washington, DC 20003
(202) 544-4259

Disciplines: foreign language (multiple user levels)

Basics and Beyond, Inc.
P.O. Box 10
Amawalk, NY 10501
(914) 962-2355

Disciplines: mathematics; spelling; geography; vocabulary;
    games (multiple user levels)

Bluebird's Computer Software
2267 23rd St.
Wyandotte, MI 48192
(313) 285-4455

Disciplines: typing; mathematics; statistical packages; games
    (multiple user levels)

The Bottom Shelf
751 Dekalb Industrial Way
Atlanta, GA 30033
(404) 296-2003

Disciplines: multiple (some educational) (multiple user level)

Computer Information Exchange
P.O. Box 159
San Luis Rey, CA 92068
(714) 757-4849

Disciplines: multiple (upper elementary–adult)

Level IV Products, Inc.
32461 Schoolcraft
Livonia, MI 48150
(313) 525-6200

Disciplines: typing; mathematics; English (multiple user levels)

Med Systems Software
P.O. Box 2674
Chapel Hill, NC 27514
(919) 942-7949

Disciplines: mathematics; money games (elementary)

MicroGnome
5843 Montgomery Rd.
Elkridge, MD 21227
(301) 796-2456

Disciplines: CAI authoring system (adult); mathematics (junior high
    school)

National Software Marketing
4701 McKinley St.
Hollywood, FL 33021
(305) 625-6062

Disciplines: accounting; computer courses (adult)

Radio Shack Education Division
1600 One Tandy Center
Fort Worth, TX 76102
(817) 390-3832

Disciplines: math (elementary–high school); language arts
    (preschool–primary)

Simutex
P.O. Box 13687
Tucson, AZ 85712
(602) 323-9391

Disciplines: games (multiple user levels)

Solartek
P.O. Box 298
Guilderland, NY 12084

Disciplines: solar energy games and simulations (multiple user
    levels)

3 R Software
P.O. Box 3115
Jamaica, NY 11431

Disciplines: language arts (elementary–junior high school)

TYC Software
40 Stuyvesant Manor
Genesco, NY 14454
(716) 243-3005

COMMODORE PET ONLY:

Comm*Data Systems
P.O. Box 325
Milford, MI 48042
(313) 685-0113

Disciplines: mathematics; geometry; English; logic; reading
    (elementary)

Prescription Learning
1301 S. Wabash Ave.
Chicago, IL 60605
(312) 922-0579

Disciplines: reading; mathematics (remedial elementary)

Teaching Tools: Microcomputer Services
P.O. Box 12679
Research Triangle Park, NC 27709
(919) 851-2374

Disciplines: addition; subtraction; spelling; matching games; letters; numbers (primary)

Tycom Associates
63 Velma Ave.
Pittsfield, MA 01201

Disciplines: algebra (multiple user levels)

TEXAS INSTRUMENTS ONLY:

Scott Foresman & Co.
1900 E. Lake Ave.
Glenview, IL 60025
(312) 729-3000

Disciplines: reading; mathematics; LOGO (grades K–primary)

SPECIAL SYSTEMS:

California Software
P.O. Box 275
El Cerrito, CA 94530
(415) 527-8717

Disciplines: COBOL and ALGOL for any CP/M-based machine (high school)

Computer Curriculum Corporation
P.O. Box 10080
Palo Alto, CA 94303
(415) 494-8450

Disciplines: reading; language arts; mathematics (multiple user levels)

Control Data Corporation
8100 34th Ave., South, P.O. Box O
Minneapolis, MN 55440
(612) 853-3541

PLATO time sharing system; run on CDC terminals

Duxbury Systems, Inc.
56 Main St.
Maynard, MA 01754
(617) 897-8207

Hardware and software sold: translates print text into braille

Gentech Corporation
4101 N. Saint Joseph Ave.
Evansville, IN 47712
(812) 423-4200

Hardware and software sold: interactive video system

Hayden Book Company, Inc.
50 Essex St.
Rochelle Park, NJ 07662
(201) 843-0550

Disciplines: mathematics

Houghton Mifflin Company
1 Beacon St.
Boston, MA 02107
(617) 725-5000

Hardware and software sold: The Answer (turnkey instructional management)

Programs for Learning
P.O. Box 954
New Milford, CT 06776
(203) 355-3452

Disciplines: chemistry (high school–college)

Science Research Associates
155 N. Wacker Dr.
Chicago, IL 60606
(800) 621-0664   (312) 984-2000 (Illinois)

Disciplines: mathematics (upper elementary–junior high school) (Classroom management system); math games

Unicom
297 Elmwood Ave.
Providence, RI 02907
(401) 467-5600

Disciplines: language; reading development

Author Index

Subject Index